100 short
poems, fiction,
& essays
with a
teacher guide

Just YA

an anthology
for grades 7-12   young   adult

love · land · world · futures · being

Editor

Sarah J. Donovan

Advisory Board

Diana Bayona
Henry "Cody" Miller
Akira Park
Robin Pelletier
Laura Swigart
Lauren Vandever
Sidra Zaheer

Publisher

Kathy Essmiller
OpenOKState
Stillwater, Oklahoma

Published in 2024 by OpenOkState, Stillwater, OK 74087

ISBN 978-1-957983-03-5

Note: This book is available for free as an Open Education Resource online at Open OkState and Ethical ELA.
https://open.library.okstate.edu/

Cover design: Sarah J. Donovan
Cover art: VinjaRindo PRatama from Pexels: Silhouette of People Jumping; Drawcee: Cityscape with Night Sky; Julia Kundova: Orange Fluffy Clouds

Praise for JUST YA

"This rich anthology of poetry, essays, and fiction showcases a range of energetic contemporary voices writing from varied and shifting perspectives, with an emphasis on currency and relevance missing from commercial textbooks. Perhaps best of all, each entry is pithy enough for discussion during even the most abbreviated class period, and the creative commons licensing allows for generous re-use for classroom teachers. An incredible resource with immediate curricular application and more than fifty pages of ideas for instructional support."

~**Wendy Stephens**, Ph.D., Associate Professor & School Library Media Program Chair, Jacksonville, Alabama

"*Just YA* is a great step forward in the movement to teach living authors. The voices in this collection speak with an authenticity that appeals to a YA audience and does not overly simplify the complexities of life, its beauty, hardships and triumphs. Overall, a thoughtful collection of works."

~ **Kate Currie**, EdD

"*Just YA* invites educators to integrate BIPOC and LGBTQ+ authors into curricula without added cost or pressure. It includes inspiring poetry, powerful short fiction, and model worthy essays, offering insights into Dr. Bishop's mirror theory and provides foundational texts for students to emulate in their writing."

~ **Carrie Mattern**, educator in Coachella Valley Desert; author of *Wakanda: Opening the High School Classroom to Afrofuturism, Coachella Valley Desert*

"This open-access collection contains a multitude of age-relevant texts that will greatly appeal to the current generation of students. From essays to fiction and poetry, this collection will be useful both for secondary students as well as professors teaching English method courses."

~**Amy Montz**, Professor of English, University of Southern Indiana, co-editor on *Adaptation on Young Adult Novels: Critically Engaging Past and Present* (Bloomsbury 2020)

More Praise for JUST YA

"*Just YA* offers adolescent students relevant and relatable perspectives on the struggle and joy of coming of age. The wide range of voices will engage students and teachers in discussions about identity and belonging to support students as they discover who they are and who they want to be."

~**Kerri Flynn**, Education Director, The Genocide Education Project

"*Just YA* offers educators and young readers a multiplicity of ways to define and understand adolescent experiences and the impact of finding your own place in the world. Educators specifically will find this collection as a practical resource to have conversations with their students about family issues, trauma, and healing."

~**Edcel Javier** Cintron-Gonzalez, Children's and YA Literature scholar & Social Media Specialist, Author of *Irma, Maria, Fiona & Me* (2023), Normal, IL

"This beautiful multigenre text is a wonderful addition to any English methods or secondary English course as the voices and writing found within are perfect examples of how creative writing of short fiction with young adults can inspire the writer in all of us."

~**T. Hunter Strickland**, co-editor on *How Young Adult Literature Gets Taught: Perspectives, Ideologies, and Pedagogical Approaches for Instruction and Assessment*

For the youth who inspire us with their stories, and for the educators who nurture their voices. May this collection spark conversations that lead to joy, understanding, and change.

Contents

JUST BEING	6
Poems	7
A Place to Breathe // Christine Hartman Derr	8
Bill-Bored // Glenda Funk	9
Pitch Black // Stacey Joy	10
Tracks // Karen J. Weyant	11
High School // Joe Bisicchia	12
North Dakota Snow Angels // Samuel Stinson	13
Zit Ode // Stefani Boutelier	14
How to Accept the Apology You Never Expected to Come // Hope Goodearl	15
Wounded Healer // Darius Phelps	16
My Voice // Melissa Heaton	17
Cracking // Karen J. Weyant	18
Bridge // Laura Shovan	19
Step Father // Emanuel Xavier	20
Hunger Is A Weapon // Federico Erebia	21
Fragments // Laura Zucca-Scott	22
Reality Bites // Rachel Toalson	23
A Sweet-Smell Memory of School // Stacey Joy	24
Psalms of My Broken Heart // Darius Phelps	25
Let Me Tell You the Truth // Rachel Toalson	26
Essays	27
On Being Armenian // Aida Zilelian	28
Up Kahuna Road // Jonathon Medeiros	31
Letter from Your New Psychiatrist // Dr. Sonia Patel	34
Family Portrait in Scars // Kayla Whaley	36
Slow Burn // Erin Murphy	38
An Indian in Yoga Class: Finding Imbalance // Rajpreet Heir	39
The Heroine // Rachel Toalson	41

Crabby Hermits and Simone Biles: Using Satire and Experimental
Forms // Carlos Greaves   42

Zilelian from Zile // Aida Zilelian   45

Fiction   48

Hot Lunch Petition // Aimee Parkison   49

The Blue Jay // Tamara Belko   50

The Reason // Val Howlett   52

This Story is Against Resilience, Supports Screaming As Needed //
Jen Ferguson   54

Spontaneous Combustion // Kristin Bartley Lenz   56

Her Story // Padma Venkatraman   59

Get Ready With Me // Taylor Byas   63

Am I Okay? // Tamara Belko   66

JUST LOVE   68

Poems   69

Daniel, My Brother // Federico Erebia   70

Runaway // Emanuel Xavier   71

landrover // Laura Kumicz   72

Between Boys // Valerie Hunter   73

Árbol // Emanuel Xavier   74

Couples Skate // Karen J. Weyant   75

Fill Me // Joe Bisicchia   76

Graduation // Chris Crowe   77

Haibun: My Girlfriend's House // Laura Shovan   78

Alienated // Emanuel Xavier   79

Essays   80

Remember // Jennifer Guyor Jowett   81

Ready // Kate Sjostrom   82

Twan't Much // Lee Martin   84

Founding Haiku Festival // Regina Harris Baiocchi   86

Fiction   89

Bittersweet // Kennedy Essmiller   90

As Petals Fall on Asphalt Roads // Aimee Parkison   93

A Decent Human // Valerie Hunter   94

Natural Selection // S Maxfield   96

Promposal // Tamara Belko   98

JUST LAND   100

  Poems   101

    Thesaurus: Word Journeys // Jennifer Guyor Jowett   102

    Pebbles in My Palm // Jamie Jo Hoang   103

    Chase // Sandra Marchetti   105

    Herencia // Alicia Partnoy   106

    Inheritance // Alicia Partnoy   107

    The Queen of Bees // Kacie Day   108

    Witness // Sandra Marchetti   109

    Erased // Erin Murphy   110

    Jibaro Dreams // Emanuel Xavier   111

    (Mapping: A Key) // Jennifer Guyor Jowett   112

    La abuela y el mar // Alicia Partnoy   113

    The Grandmother and the Sea // Alicia Partnoy 114

  Essays   115

    Living Near St. Catherine School // Jonathon Medeiros   116

    Stupid Girls // Jen Ferguson   118

    Swinging // Karen J. Weyant   120

  Fiction   121

    Lights Out // Brittany Saulnier   122

    The Stillness of Flight // David Schaafsma   124

    The Listener // Aimee Parkison   127

JUST WORLD   128

  Poems   129

    Moonscape // Zetta Elliott   130

    Juneteenth is Not Freedom // Stacey Joy   131

    Girls' Playground, Harriet Island, St. Paul, MN (1905) // Jennifer Guyor Jowett   132

    Belonging // Joe Bisicchia   133

We Gather Here Together // Rachel Toalson   134

Just Word(le) // Jennifer Guyor Jowett   135

Family Stories // Mary E. Cronin   136

There Must Be a Gate // Laura Shovan   137

I Refuse to Be Underestimated // Rachel Toalson   138

Unconstitutional // Stacey Joy   139

Peace Play // Linda Mitchell   140

Essays   141

Irish Whistle // Kate Sjostrom   142

Fiction   144

Feathers // Valerie Hunter   145

Hunterlore // Dana Claire   148

Drive-by (In Three Acts) // Jennifer Guyor Jowett   149

JUST FUTURES   152

Poems   153

Chasing the American Dream // Laura Zucca-Scott   154

We Need Stories // Jennifer Guyor Jowett   155

Envision // Joe Bisicchia   156

A Remembrance // Rachel Toalson   157

Illuminated // Erin Murphy   158

Star Gatherers // Jennifer Guyor Jowett   159

Word of the day: Techwright // Stefani Boutelier   160

Don't Call Me A Robot // Laura Shovan   161

For Sale: M1k0 the Robot // Laura Shovan   162

MessageChatGPT // Linda Mitchell   163

Things Just Don't Work Like They Used To // Darius Phelps   164

Essays   165

A Vision for Inclusive Campuses: Balancing Comfort and Conflict Through Dialogue //Alana Mondschein   166

Compulsory Service // S.   169

Fiction   170

My Jam Jar Ghost// Shih-Li Kow   171

TEACHER GUIDE   173

   How to Use This Book   174

   Pair Share   177

   Characterization: Place Poem   179

   Tone of Just Being   181

   Justice Literature Circles   184

   Reading Poetry Relationally   193

   Choice Reading with Reading Conferences   197

   The Answer to Vocabulary Instruction   201

   Four Quarters of Choice Reading: A Progression   207

   Vlogging as Embodied Reading Response   219

Appendix   226

About the Editor   231

About the Advisory Board   239

Introduction

by Sarah J. Donovan

Being a student in today's high school is the same as it ever was, but it is also completely unrecognizable. Two things can be true. The same novels and plays of decades past are still "covered" in paperless classrooms where students compose on keyboards or phones rather than (or along with) paper and pen. Some students walk school hallways to get to class while others opt for distance learning and may never step foot in a classroom again.

And yet across the physical and digital spaces of school and social media, students are getting quite a different education about our world, lessons not always acknowledged, but essential to understanding how we are shaped and can shape our world. In our junior and high school classrooms, how many of the textbooks and required novels feature contemporary youth's lived experiences? Not many.

Just YA: Short Poems, Essays, & Fiction for Grades 7-12 is a collection of open licensed, non-revenue seeking literature about inclusive, affirming, justice-oriented ways of being and the incredible capacity of youth, *intentionally* curated for classrooms. This collection is thematic, short, free, open-licensed, and youth-centered.

Thematic

Just YA is organized in themes around identity, love, land, world, and futures (see Table 1) that we see in conversation with the required canonical texts and youth interests. The forms (poetry, essay, and narrative) are selected to inspire student writing, including *creative* fiction and nonfiction. Of course, we see all writing as creative, but literary analysis or text-dependent writing seems to dominate secondary writing curricula. We hope educators will use these youth-focused texts to update their curriculum and shift their conceptual unit framing to consider contemporary youth perspectives and how *Just YA* texts can inspire students to write their own poems, creative nonfiction essays, and flash fiction.

In each section, there are multiple texts around the same topic to foster rich discussions in the classroom. Consider these text sets around which an entire unit could be developed. The texts are written by diverse adult authors, considering geography, class, race, language, religion, gender, sexuality, and ability. Multilingual authors draw on their entire linguistic repertoire to celebrate linguistic diversity.

Table 1. *Just YA* Themes

Just Being: A focus on complex ways of being, including mental health, nourishment, embodied diversities, wellbeing, trauma, healing, play, work, rest, faith, and spirituality
Just Love: A focus on all the ways of love and loving: romance, familial, friendship, self, dating, divorce, blended families, and found family. These writers consider all the ways of showing love and what is just, equitable, and sustaining about healthy love
Just Land: A focus on ways that place shapes us and we shape place: land rights, land use, fires, deforestation, farming, gentrification, housing (in)equity, unhoused communities, climate justice, relationships with nature-water-air, rurality, urbanity, and (de)coloniality
Just World: An exploration of joy, peace, justice, war and stories of travel, culture,, art, language, politics, faith, connectivity, policies, and places
Just Futures: A focus on ways of navigating and imagining technologies, AI, robots, space travel/occupation, medicine, education, science, dreaming, healthcare and just futures in being, love, land, and the world

Short

In my work in teacher education and professional development over the past decade, I found that teachers were spending a lot of time searching for short texts to study and enjoy with students. Go to any Facebook teacher group, and you will find teachers searching for a short story to teach theme or a poem to study symbolism. I love young adult anthologies and often enjoy them in my college young adult literature courses. I even had entire shelf of anthologies in my junior high classroom. And I drew on short fiction authors to help me teacher writing (e.g., leads, dialogue, and sensory language lessons). However, some anthology stories can ten or twenty pages, which is too long to read in a class period of 45 minutes. To understand theme or the evolution of a symbol in a text, readers have to read the whole story, which could take days.

Free and Open

And then, of course, there is the concern of copyright infringement and funding. To purchase a class set of an anthology could cost hundreds of dollars out of a teacher's pocket. I am sure you have seen and contributed to teachers' Amazon lists and Go Fund Me projects. Many teachers self-funding their classrooms, investing money year after year to keep up with new trends and publications. Thus, this project evolved out of a teacher-need for short texts that are for teens, beautifully written, free, and with open licensing.

All the content is free to readers and available online, in PDF, or a paperback copy (which may incur a profit for the bookstore). While many books say "no part of this book may be reproduced in any form without permission," we ask that you *do* reproduce, store, share, copy, distribute any and all of it in the classroom and beyond! We *want* these in the hearts and hands of youth across the world. Authors have generously made them available to readers for free.

This collection is licensed as an Open Education Resource (OER) CC BY-NC-ND 4.0. This means that individual authors retain copyright of their work. You must give appropriate credit, provide a link to the license. If you remix, transform, or build upon the material, you may not distribute the modified material without permission from the author.

Youth-Centered

To develop this collection, we began by inviting young adult authors whose work we have shared in our own classrooms to contribute a short text to the anthology: Padma Venkatraman, Zetta

Elliott, Jen Ferguson, Federico Erebia, and Chris Crowe among others. We reached out to well-known flash fiction and flash creative nonfiction writers from *Brevity* (e.g., Rajpreet Heir, Erin Murphy, Lee Martin) because flash fiction is not a form that has made it to young adult literature publishers yet (or not that we knew of). Finally, we invited teacher-poets to contribute short poems, essays, and fiction. Teachers are writers, too, and we feature many incredible educator-authors in this anthology such as Stacey Joy, Jennifer Guyor Jowett, Glenda Funk, and Tamara Belko (among others).

Inclusive & Affirming

Of all our authors, we asked that they craft inclusive stories that dispel stereotypes of youth and represent agentive youth characters so that our students can see themselves in the school literature curriculum. With an advisory board of young adult literature (YAL) scholars, secondary teachers, and secondary students, we've curated this collection to spark deep conversations in classrooms (and beyond) about the literary merit of short form literature with "universal" themes that center youth stories. The poems, essays, and fiction offered here and in paperback show the ways youth demand, enact, and deserve literature that shows them just, equitable, joyful lives. Together, the advisory board developed a framework for selecting texts. See Table 2. Our hope is that this criteria may support educators as they consider the youth representation in their curriculum and reading lives.

Support

In addition to the rich collection of poems, flash fiction, and essays, this anthology includes a valuable resource at the end called the "Teacher Guide." This section offers a variety of lesson ideas and strategies designed to help educators integrate these texts into their classrooms effectively. The Teacher Guide aims to provide insights and support from my fifteen years of experience teaching secondary students with young adult literature. The goal is to enhance English language arts teaching practice with strategies that support literary comprehension, critical reading, and the enjoyment of literature, fostering a rich and engaging learning environment for all students.

In the Appendix online is a table of the poems, essays, and fiction by title, author, form, and theme. You can search and sort this table to find the texts you are looking to shape your curriculum or for reading joy.

Table 2. *Just YA* text selection framework

Just YA Text Selection	
Diversity	Multiple intersections of identity in the text or through the author bio implied (gender, class, sexuality, race, culture, language, religion, geography, ability, body, mental health)
Equity	Joy, positive representations, asset-based rather than only harm, victim hood, no deficit-based language
Youth-relevant	For ages 12-18, not adult focused; youth are at the center or there is something early adulthood that young adults can stretch into, benefit from without talking down to youth or lecturing; avoid didactic stories & essays
Language	Accessible for a range of youth, beautiful, translanguaging, regional dialects used affirmatively; no cursing as it will be in schools; slurs or harmful language is used with care and intentionality for healing rather than shock or harm
Message	May or may not be a message; joy is enough; relevant to youth; sophisticated rather than cliché or talking down to youth; exploring themes of love, being, land, futures, world, etc.
Length	Short, one page poem; under 1,000 words story/essay

Just Being

poetry· flash fiction · essays

Just poetry

love land world futures being

A Place to Breathe // Christine Hartman Derr

Off the path,
        behind some trees,
a clearing sits
        and waits for me.
A forest symphony,
        a place for finding tohi.
                    Here
          I can simply be   simply breathe,
            find a way
            back to me.

           Those hateful words,
        that awful silence
      recedes in waves
    until it's quiet.

The clouds drift by   the sun softens   leaves whisper comforting words
        a language maybe I used to know.

"Wado, detlugv," I thank the trees.
        Next the grass, the bees.
"Wado, ganolvvsgv,"
      gratitude for wind, for breezes.
"Wado, unelvnvhi,"
      gratitude in a whisper to Creator
      for feeling wrapped in that precious, neverending ancestor love
      for this world, this clearing, this moment.
A twig snaps
      Two pairs of eyes
        watch me, watching them.

      A doe and her fawn
hover on the edge of the small clearing.
      They take me in,
      weigh my soul–
then stay,
nibbling at a bush.

They feel safe.
      So do I.

            That's when I know
            we'll be alright.

Christine Hartman Derr is a citizen of the Cherokee Nation of Oklahoma. She holds a Master of Fine Arts in Writing for Children & Young Adults from the Vermont College of Fine Arts. She runs the website PawPrintsInTheSink.com and is a contributor to an upcoming YA anthology from Heartdrum.

Bill-Bored // Glenda Funk

bored bill
yawn spilled

nodded off
assignment scoffed

played games
teacher blamed

watched TikTok
work forgot

excuses made
graduation delayed

mom sad
dad mad

second chance
old rant

moral tale—
unholy grail

seize day
don't delay

Glenda Funk taught English and speech communication. She serves on NCTE's Children's Poetry Awards Committee. Her poetry is featured in *Teacher-Poets Writing to Bridge the Distance: An Oral History of COVID-19 in Poems* and *Rhyme and Rhythm: Poems for Student Athletes*. Glenda has written for *California English* and blogs at *Swirl & Swing:* www.glendafunk.wordpress.com

Pitch Black // Stacey Joy

In the pitch blackness of our skin
Is an ocean waving in diamonds
Stories written in gold
Skies raining in silk

Is an ocean waving in diamonds
Where tsunamis of torture die
Skies raining in silk
Healing our bones and blood

Where tsunamis of torture die
In the pitch blackness of our skin
Healing our bones and blood
Stories written in gold

Stacey Joy is a National Board Certified Teacher who has taught for 38 years in Los Angeles. Stacey is a self-published poet and has poems published in various anthologies: *Out of Anonymity, Savant Poetry Anthologies, Teacher Poets Writing to Bridge the Distance,* and *Rhythm and Rhyme: Poems for Student Athletes.*

Tracks // Karen J. Weyant

Trains have not used these tracks for years.
    Still, I lean down to feel the trembling,
but all I feel is frozen steel,
    cold from melted February snow.

Still, I lean down to feel the trembling,
    like the dance of pennies on shaking rails,
cold from melted February snow,
    waiting for the rumblings of railway boxcars.

Like the dance of pennies on shaking rails,
    I feel something like a shiver.
Waiting for the rumblings of railway boxcars,
    I know the weight of homesickness.

I feel something like a shiver
    from the scratch of winter's edge.
I know the weight of homesickness
    is an ache that makes it hard to breathe.

From the scratch of winter's edge,
    I almost believe that I could bleed from what
is an ache that makes it hard to breathe.
    I pull my coat tight around me.

I almost believe that I could bleed from what
    I feel is frozen steel.
I pull my coat tight around me.
    Trains have not used these tracks for years.

Karen J. Weyant's first full-length collection, *Avoiding the Rapture* was published last fall by Riot in Your Throat press. Her poems have appeared in *Crab Orchard Review, Copper Nickel, Harpur Palate, Fourth River, Lake Effect, Rattle, River Styx* and *Slipstream*. She lives, reads and writes in Northern Pennsylvania but is an Associate Professor of English at Jamestown Community College in Jamestown, New York.

High School // Joe Bisicchia

To be, or not
to be somewhat fascinating.
I won't always be
boorish, sophomoric.
Soon, I'll be a junior and then
a senior and carry myself
with proper erudite demeanor.
Here I am experiencing the ages
firsthand. Beyond the books,
within the geometry circles,
it all comes alive. Yes, the ages
have long been alive. And I am
part of it, as if this is the way
of all time. So, I'm pleased
to sit with Lincoln at lunch.
His beard, while eating pizza,
at first a distraction. But then
I feel my own cheese sloppily
on my own chin. Ah, my own
early mozzarella of wisdom.

Joe Bisicchia has nearly four decades of experience in language arts, from journalism and broadcasting, to teaching, marketing, public affairs, and poetry. An Honorable Mention recipient for the Fernando Rielo XXXII World Prize for Mystical Poetry, he has written four published collections of poetry.

North Dakota Snow Angels // Samuel Stinson

Take me out there
Take me out when it is fifteen below
And we are wearing five layers of warm flannel
And outside--show me the northern lights
Point out the north star
Point to the silent winter stars
That blue sky that darkens so late in summer
That dark sky now, that now beams down that bright curtain light
Take me out there now
Take me out now to the snowbank, away from the blowing drifts
To the fresh three feet of untouched snow
To the spot where we lie, brushing our arms up and around
With white wings

Samuel Stinson began developing an interest in writing after he began reading the novels of R.A. Salvatore in 1994. These days, Samuel teaches English and writes for a variety of publications. His most recent publication is Embodied Environmental Risk in Technical Communication, co-edited with Mary Le Rouge.

Zit Ode // Stefani Boutelier

O, your *eruption*
glistening in the light
illuminating *puss* in a
blackhead, whitehead
ring of *rosacea*
satisfying, disgusting
you visit all, fully inclusive
you are famous, loved, hated
yet a sign, *cyst, blister*
you help identify
bacteria, puberty
food, ill hygiene
we humanize you
as you grow
celebrate you even
you've *oozed* your
way into *pop* media
in so many personalities
by so many names
pimple, blemish, acne
boil, bump, welt
O, thee *blain* of
my face's existence

Stefani Boutelier, Ph.D., is an Associate Professor of Education at Aquinas College in Michigan. She teaches courses for pre-service and in-service teachers focused on instructional design, diverse literacy, technology integration, and research methods. Her K-12 teaching was in Southern California before moving into teacher preparation.

How to Accept the Apology You Never Expected to Come //
Hope Goodearl

Have you ever had an experience that just cracked every piece of you, down to your core? Something that you never expected, like being sucker punched in the gut. You didn't know how it happened. You didn't know if you should fight to fix it right away, But then realized, It wasn't your job to fix it. It was the person who took the swing.

So, what do you do when the apology you never expected to come finally arrives?

1. Take a moment to live in the shock. It's okay. I give you permission.
2. ~~Avoid reading it like the plague.~~
    a. Scratch that. Covid shows that humans are incapable of avoiding a literal plague.
3. Avoid it like you avoided your least favorite relative at family gatherings.
4. Stare at the notification that won't go away until you read or mark the message as read.
5. Take a moment (or a few) to process that they actually sent a message that is likely the apology you never thought you would receive.
6. Ignore it for as many days as you need to decide if you want to read it or not.
7. Talk to a trusted friend about your feelings. Even if they don't know what to say to help, talking it out might be all that you need.
8. Take the time to decide if you're ready to hear an apology.
9. Take time to decide if you want the apology or to just move on.
10. Stare at the notification some more.
11. Decide what you want to come out of the apology. Is it the same as when everything happened? Are you reading just to let the person know you heard their apology?
12. Take a deep breath.
13. Read the apology.
14. Take another breath.
15. Continue moving forward.

Hope Goodearl is a high school English teacher with a love for creative writing of all aspects, even if she has a love-hate relationship with poetry. She has previously published 6 other poems to various journals and magazines with the hope of one day publishing a full-length novel.

Wounded Healer // Darius Phelps

I couldn't kill
my rage,
so I tried to kill
the parts of you
within me,
instead.

Just because I don't
have your last name,
I've come to realize
we are still
one and the same.

I know that
I possess venom
that spills
from your
bloodline.

There is mania
inside of me,
and from it
I refuse to flee.

Let this pain,
this trauma,
consume me
and part my soul
like the
Red
Sea.

No matter how much
I've fasted and prayed
these demons
are here
to stay.

I am a wounded healer
and I know
I will be okay.

Darius Phelps is a PhD candidate at Teachers College, Columbia University. An educator, poet, spoken word artist, and activist, Darius writes poems about grief, liberation, emancipation, and reflection through the lens of a teacher of color, as well as experiencing Black boy joy.

My Voice // Melissa Heaton

My voice is timid
Shrinking from criticism
Seeking acceptance

Hiding under the
Covers of imperfection
Longing to wake up

There are moments when
I come to myself and rise
With clear perspective

My slumbering voice
comes alive. I'm empowered.
Uninhibited

My true self stands tall
Shaking off the dust of doubt.
Honest. Bold. Fearless.

My words are enough
Letting go, my voice takes flight
Finally, I'm me.

Melissa Heaton has taught for 24 years and currently teaches 8th grade English at Mapleton Jr. High School in Nebo School District. She is an active fellow of the Central Utah Writing Project. When she is not teaching or writing, Melissa enjoys baking, reading, and traveling to national parks.

Cracking // Karen J. Weyant

Every kitchen edge was her tool:
the side of the sink, a rim
of a mixing bowl, the round lip
of a measuring cup. Snapping
her wrist my mother could break
an egg with a single flick, pull apart
shells so that a stray thumb
would never slip into the yolk.
Yellow suns like those
in my crayon-colored pictures
fell into frying pans or mixing bowls.
Circles were never punctured,
but with every toss of broken shell,
her skin grew thinner. Veins bulged,
deep fate lines cut into her hands.
This is where I learned that
a clean break starts with a tiny
fracture, and then a crack.

Karen J. Weyant's first full-length collection, *Avoiding the Rapture* was published last fall by Riot in Your Throat press. Her poems have appeared in *Crab Orchard Review, Copper Nickel, Harpur Palate, Fourth River, Lake Effect, Rattle, River Styx* and *Slipstream*. She lives, reads and writes in Northern Pennsylvania but is an Associate Professor of English at Jamestown Community College in Jamestown, New York.

Bridge // Laura Shovan

Since I picked up the guitar, listening to music's
not the same. My brain hears patterns. Verse chorus
verse chorus   bridge   chorus, fade.

My teacher says the bridge is where a song
takes risks, steps onto the Road Less Traveled.
"Yeah, man," I say. "I get it. Robert Frost."
He grins, cues up an Ozzy tune, plays lead
along with Randy Rhoads. Driving, writhing strums
push Ozzy's wails of "I don't know."

I don't know either, Oz. I'm almost eighteen.
Almost done with high school.
When people ask what I'm doing next year,
I want to scream, "I don't know."

"Here it comes," my guitar teacher says.
A bit of bass and then, everything s l o w s.

                    Randy Rhoads

fills the practice room. The bridge. A change
in rhythm, dynamics, a path to the song's culmination.

I don't know what my bridge is.
The only song I know goes: school work
school work college work   f a d e   o u t.

Laura Shovan is a Pushcart Prize-nominated poet and a middle grade novelist. Among her award-winning children's books are *The Last Fifth Grade of Emerson Elementary*, *Takedown*, and *A Place at the Table*, written with Saadia Faruqi. Laura is a longtime poet-in-the-schools. She teaches at Vermont College of Fine Arts.

Step Father // Emanuel Xavier

He forgets that he used to call me *mariconcito* —
that I harbored years of hatred toward him
while hoping to find my real father. My
childhood memories of him reminding me
I was my mother's son, not his. I tried
to poison him once and scattered sharp nails
inside the shoes in his closet. By the time one
of his sons died of AIDS, I was already lost
in contempt for the man I blamed for everything.
There was the time I was in love and he met my
boyfriends. Now he forgets to go to the bathroom
or where he is. I help him walk slowly
outdoors to step outside the prison cell that is
the tiny apartment with no windows in which
I grew up abused by both of them. He barely
understands. His fate has been torture. I know
that I cannot be his savior. I used to pray for
him to die but here he is slowly fading. In his
eyes I see that he learned to love me and wishes
he could take it all back. He is unable to recall
those drunken nights and hateful words. I should
do the same. I left a long time ago but he still
remains haunted by the little boy who wanted
to belong. Like him, I want to forget that we
made mistakes and caused so much pain. I need
for both of us to remember how he taught me
how to ride a bike and how to swim and told
me, better late than never, that he loved me and
was proud of all I had done. I have to help him
settle into his favorite chair and let him know that
I forgive him. There is a place somewhere where
he will call me *hijo* and I will know him as my dad.

Emanuel Xavier is author of several poetry books including *Selected Poems of Emanuel Xavier* and *Love(ly) Child*. His books have been finalists for International Latino Book Awards and Lambda Literary Awards and his work has appeared in Poetry, A Gathering of the Tribes, Best American Poetry, and elsewh

Hunger Is A Weapon // Federico Erebia

An excerpt from *Pedro & Daniel* (Levine Querido 2023)

Hunger is a weapon.

The physical and emotional sickness of hunger
is unfathomable to the fortunate.
I was not so fortunate.
Cafeteria Christians at their biblican buffet
would deny children meals in schools.
- Others would use hunger to bend another to their will.

Hunger is a weapon.

The hunger for love is human,
The hunger for ac-cep-tance is human,
The hunger for community is human,
The hunger for meaning is human,
The hunger for power is human.

Hunger is a weapon.

Hunger for knowledge is formidable
against other weapons.
It was my "ticket out of town."
Knowledge is mine,
Hidden,
Where no one can see it,
Where no one can find it,
Where no one can take it,
Where I can wield it.

Federico Erebia, a retired physician, woodworker, author, poet, and illustrator, is the recipient of the 2024 Lambda Literary Award for Exceptional New Writer. His debut novel, *Pedro & Daniel* (Levine Querido 2023), has received awards and other critical acclaim. He lives in Massachusetts with his husband. Visit https://FJEbooks.com for more details.

Fragments // Laura Zucca-Scott

I am listening to the fragments of your stories
Once they were fluid and brought me back to
a world I had never known
to my grandfather's story
I had longed to hear for a long time
When you finally decided I was ready
or maybe you were, you started telling me
all I needed to know to be myself
I saw a remote village wounded by the war
I smelled the acrid smoke of destruction and fear
I heard people crying in desperation
I tried to wipe tears away from a child's face
I felt the sunshine on the beach
and the sea healing the pain
with the hopes and freedom of youth
But now the fragments pull apart
and I am trying to bring the images
back together. I am mourning for the losses
yet to come. I am hoping for a future we can still build

Laura Zucca-Scott, Ph.D., is a bilingual writer and educator. Her works have been published in English and Italian. Recently, her work was featured in the North Dakota Quarterly. In December 2023, she was the recipient of the Third Prize of the International Literary Prize, "Florence, Capital of Europe," Italy.

Reality Bites // Rachel Toalson

We used to play it
on the cement slab,
four squares marked out,
grass growing between the lines

We tried not to pay attention
to the world around us
We were girls
just trying to have fun

But that's where Jesse R.
humped the air and
whistled at us
and it's where Mario C.
told Adona she had nice knockers
and it's where Brandon H.
cut in and said, *I've got something*
you can play with if you're
getting bored with Four Square

We chased them off,
but they always came back,
        leering

I was eight years old
when I learned
I was not a girl
just trying to have fun
I would never be a girl
just trying to have fun

I was a body on display
for the fun of the
world

Rachel Toalson is the author of *The Colors of the Rain, The Woods, The First Magnificent Summer,* and *Something Maybe Magnificent* (Simon& Schuster, 2024). Her poetry has been published in print magazines and literary journals around the world. She lives in San Antonio, Texas, with her husband and six sons.

A Sweet-Smell Memory of School // Stacey Joy

Seven years old
chalk in my right hand
a key ring full of stinky old keys in my other hand
whistle on yarn ready for blowing

My miniature chalkboard
propped against my headboard
leaving sufficient sitting space
for my dolls to learn in rows

Encyclopedia "M" open to the page on mammals
that week's spelling list in perfect manuscript on chart paper
addition equations on flash cards in pungent blue marker
all prepped and ready for "class" to begin

Some days I dressed up in Mommy's orange blazer
with a paisley scarf around my neck
red lipstick and pink nail polish
"Good morning, class. My name is Miss Johnson."

15 years later, I wore my First Day of School clothes,
had two classroom keys that smelled like power
and a new box of colored chalk
releasing the aroma of possibility

Stacey Joy is a National Board Certified Teacher who has taught for 38 years in Los Angeles. Stacey is a self-published poet and has poems published in various anthologies: *Out of Anonymity, Savant Poetry Anthologies, Teacher Poets Writing to Bridge the Distance,* and *Rhythm and Rhyme: Poems for Student Athletes.*

Psalms of My Broken Heart // Darius Phelps

I open the windows
to the psalms of my broken heart
knowing that
my grief
embedded words
won't resonate
with many.
But, there is something about
the sweet release of my bated breath
fogging up my view of what lies ahead
as the lingering summer rain trickles down
reminding me that pain -- *this pain*
is only temporary.
crying out from –
the psalms of my broken heart,
He stares at me in amazement
wondering how these scars
have molded me into this
man that reaches with the
outstretched hand
I have found myself buried
in these trauma bond trenches
I now know
that this
grief garden
is where I
belong.
This is where
the rebirth
starts.

Darius Phelps is a PhD candidate at Teachers College, Columbia University. An educator, poet, spoken word artist, and activist, Darius writes poems about grief, liberation, emancipation, and reflection through the lens of a teacher of color, as well as experiencing Black boy joy.

Let Me Tell You the Truth // Rachel Toalson

people call me brave / I am not brave / I am burning / the fire has nowhere to go / but up / the blaze of my being / incinerated / to produce / an offering of truth

people call me admirable / I am not admirable / I am unable / to stay silent / in the face of injustice / a character flaw at times / a strength at others

people call me prolific / I am not prolific / my body is not strong enough / to hold all the words /inside / they gallop out / into the world / instead

people call me noble / I am not noble / I merely believe / we are all human / all connected / all on an equal plane / of worth / significance / potential

people call me wise / I am not wise / I only know what it is / to lie / at the bottom of the world /and wonder / if I'll ever get back up / and so / I try / to remember / how to fly

Rachel Toalson is the author of *The Colors of the Rain, The Woods, The First Magnificent Summer,* and *Something Maybe Magnificent* (Simon& Schuster, 2024). Her poetry has been published in print magazines and literary journals around the world. She lives in San Antonio, Texas, with her husband and six sons.

Just essays

love land world futures being

On Being Armenian // Aida Zilelian

I was in my 7th grade social studies class and we had just completed a geography unit on Europe and the Middle East. I was sitting in my usual seat in the back row listening to my teacher Mrs. Barone talk about the coming events after the new year.

"We're going to have a cultural celebration," she explained, "and I will be asking each of you to bring in a dish from your country of origin."

I noted the date and decided I would feign illness the night before.

"Now let's go around the room and share our country of origin, even if your parents are third or fourth generation."

I watched as my classmates stood up one by one. Italy. Germany. Russia. Israel. Korea. When it was my turn I stood up and mumbled, "Armenia."

"You have to speak up, Aida. We can't hear you from all the way in the back."

It wouldn't have made a difference if I had said it through a loud speaker. "Armenia."

My classmates looked at each other wonderingly, as if I had created a mythical land. They snickered. I heard one of them say, "Arma – who?"

It was the same face they made when I unpacked my lunch in the cafeteria, where I endured their imaginative and crude speculations of what I was eating.

"What *is* that?" someone had once asked, conveying the table's collective revulsion.

"Dolma," I had said.

I had looked down at the meat-stuffed zucchini covered in garlicky yogurt and sumac, realizing the question was more a declaration of disgust.

The anonymity of my origin followed me everywhere. Most adults had never heard of Armenia.

"Albanian?" someone once asked.

"No," I said. "Armenian."

"Where is that?"

Patiently, I would explain that we were part of the Soviet Republic. I wanted to tell them that historically, we were the first people to accept Christianity as a religion. That our first churches were built in the fourth century. That the Genocide in 1915 had orphaned my grandfather, and my father's side of the family consisted of my grandmother, my aunt and my father. When I peered at the map hanging in my bedroom I saw the small speck of land, the size of a fingernail bordered in the center of Turkey, Iran and Azerbaijan. We wouldn't claim independence until 1991.

"Don't forget that you are a Zilelian!" my father would say.

He was practically fanatical, his obsession with our family name and Armenian heritage. Feeling invisible by the world, his emphatic stance seemed overblown and embarrassing.

Worse still was explaining to people the turn of the century Genocide during World War I and the Turkish government's denial of murdering nearly two-million Armenians. If no one knew what Armenia was, how would this crime against humanity, against my people ever be recognized? I did not feel marginalized, overlooked, discriminated against. I felt as if I did not exist.

I looked through books about the Genocide that my father had purchased from the Armenian Prelacy, turning each page over with the realization that my father's aunts, uncles, relatives had all been killed. Pictures of the barren Syrian desert and a long procession of Armenians on a death march. Disembodied heads placed on shelves as if on display. Skeletal bodies in a heaping pile in a mass grave. Images of the front pages of the New York Times: *Million Armenians Killed or In Exile, Armenians Sent to Perish in Desert* - it would all plague me. The world had looked on silently and done nothing. And nearly a hundred years later, it seemed no one knew who we were, who I was.

Adding to my hollow sense of identity was another layer that would alienate me from my peers: I was first-generation Armenian. To a passive onlooker, this would not mean all that much. But to me it meant being deprived of joys that felt significant. That I did not go trick-or-treating. *I'm not sending you to strangers' homes begging for candy.* There were no sleepovers. *You have your own bed to sleep in, you don't need to sleep anywhere else.* I was discouraged from having American friends. *You can play with your sister and your cousins* (who all lived out of state). Chinese takeout was out of the question.

They're goal was not to isolate me anymore than I already was, but to protect me from a fate that was equivalent to death: marrying an *odar* – an American. Ironically, the word means out of place, unfamiliar. And it's the feeling that consumed me for most of my upbringing. Looking back, I wonder if my parents realized the naïveté of their expectations. I attended Armenian elementary school five days a week, followed by Armenian Saturday school and Sunday school at the Armenian church in Manhattan. I didn't realize it then, but I was suffocating.

Looking back, there were glimmers of happiness that I experienced. The Festival of Grapes, which was held annually in Astoria's Bohemian Hall. There, we all came together and danced, ate, ran around with friends as Armenian music blared through the speakers. The bara-hanteses – dinner dances were a splendid thing. Platters of food crowding our dinner table, the noise and chatter of people speaking Armenian, the live band bringing to life the albums my parents played on Sunday afternoons. We were a clan, orphaned by tragedy.

It wasn't until years after my parents' scandalous divorce and remarrying that I was able to break away from my community. I married an American and had one child. I wrote a novel which received an award funded by an Armenian foundation. At my book signing I stood in awe at the sight of all the Armenians, many of whom I did not know personally, who had come to support me. They were there because I was one of them. They didn't need to know me. I remember their beaming faces sitting in the crowd, how proud they seemed that an Armenian had written a book and it was being celebrated.

After the event many of them approached me to extend their congratulations. I was ashamed suddenly that I had turned away from my Armenian culture.

The distance of decades since my adolescence has come full circle in my realizations. I understand that I am part of an ancient history, a small and mighty tribe. And that we are not fragile. We defied the age-old cliché of reigning strength in numbers. We didn't just survive. We live.

Aida Zilelian is a first generation American-Armenian writer, educator and storyteller from Queens, NY. She is the author of *The Legacy of Lost Things* (2015, Bleeding Heart Publications) which was the recipient of the 2014 Tololyan Literary Award. Aida's most recent novel, *All the Ways We Lied,* released in January 2024 (Keylight Books/Turner Bookstore).

Up Kahuna Road // Jonathon Medeiros

I did not grow up on the farm. We weren't allowed to live there, a stipulation of the lease from the state. I was raised there, though. The farm raised me. I spent parts of every day there for 10 years, spanning the ages of 7-17. When I moved away for college, so many tacked together pieces of our family, the farm included, began to fall apart.

Can I describe the farm, even? What is it now? What does it mean to tell someone about the farm, a place that no longer exists, barely ever did?

I can start with facts: The farm is (was) up on Kahuna Road, with Pantalon's dirt road wrapping the other side. There is a river there, Kapa'a Stream, and a valley, also the random decaying foundations of buildings I have never seen but often imagined, and also the old bunker on the hill. Makaleha stands over the valley, the river, the farm. It is green and black and brown, tall, dripping mist into waterfalls into the stream down in the valley on its way to the ocean.

The farm is a physical place still, though few people know it as the place that I mean. The farm is something else also, surrounded not by roads and landmarks but by 10 years marked on a timeline in the minds of five people, with hurricanes on either side. It is a phrase that calls to reality a place, a time, a dragging, sucking, sick sunny raining feeling filled with goats, post holes, and the piling of rocks.

We built a barn or it was already there. We fortified and tended the pigpens, the goat corrals. We tilled the soil and moved the rocks. We bent and twisted barbed and hog and electric wire around the edges and the interiors of the layers of the 10 acres of the farm. I hammered bent nails straight, taking them from one bucket to another. I sorted nuts and bolts and washers, tried to avoid getting fingers caught in the vegetable washer, mixed and sprayed gallons of weed-killer, no gloves no mask no adult supervision.

I remember a massive mud puddle, near the first barn. We played in the puddle often, with gi joes and hot wheels. We searched for and avoided the toads and their pearl string laces of eggs. When the sun shone for days, the puddle dried and captured our toys along with the toads; all were excavated after each heavy rain by our small searching hands, tender from youth and not yet living life.

There was an old tub, maybe two, outside the pigpen where Sarah sat to scold the sows and piglets. When I pulled prawns from the river I set them in the tubs and installed automatic water fillers and air circulators; the water turned black anyway and I don't know what we did with all the prawns and o'opu I put there.

The burn pile was near the pigpens and tubs, part way down the hill where the road wrapped around a steep outcropping bringing tractors to the valley and the river. We burned so many things. Feed bags, rotted lumber, tin cans, batteries, tires, dead goats, limbs from fallen albizia trees, old fireworks and shotgun shells. The smoke carried away on the wind but the smell lingers. The smoke lifted, black with diesel and dead animals and tire rubber, billowing up, offending the blue skies and Makaleha's green cliffs. We never burned enough though to really get rid of all the filth. That followed us to other storage places, forgotten until something tumbles down on our heads when we open a door, hear a certain sound, utter a specific word or question.

We always had goats. Henry, Henrietta, Mama, Daisy, and the others. Some of these we killed for our neighbors, tying them up, draining their blood at the throat so their screams turned to wet gargling as the bucket filled. We exchanged these animals for the sausage from the blood and entrails. We often had chickens. These we hung from their feet so that I could open their throats with a buck knife, their white and yellow heads turning red then black. I asked my dad about what my teacher said at recess, that we ran around like chickens with our heads cut off. In answer, he took one to the huge stump in the barnyard, slapped it down and chopped its head off in a flash. The now un capitated bird flopped and wiggled but disappointingly did not run.

One year, the valley was full of sweet corn, taller than me and my sister. One year, the rocky front pasture filled with marigold, thousands of them, deep red and orange, a blanket from fence line to fence line. For a birthday once, we laid out a bunch of old tarps on the hillside in the horse paddock. We twisted all the hoses together to reach from the barn to the top of the tarp and let the water flow, rain water from Makaleha actually, or so the county always tells us. The makeshift slip n slide worked but the rocks under the grass still pierced the fabric and eventually our skin. I remember the rocks; I remember the message communicated to the gathered friends by those tarps when I think about that birthday.

After the second hurricane, the first barn fell on the land cruiser. We built a new one, closer to the valley's edge, closer to the papaya and overlooking the sweet corn, the curve of the river peaking through hau bush and lantana, like the curves of the woman I often nervously watched at Kealia while I was learning about surfing and women.

And what is down there now, in the valley, near the river, under the tree cover of jungle? Friends, loneliness, days spent, prawn traps, mud, coconut meat, moss and rock dams, Pantalon's dead wife, orange and green sludge in the slow corners of the overflow channels. And what is there now?

River rock. Silt. Water. Me. Some part of me.

Jonathon Medeiros, former director of the Kaua'i Teacher Fellowship, has been teaching and learning about Language Arts and rhetoric for nearly 20 years with students on Kaua'i and he frequently writes about education, equity, and the power of curiosity. He believes in teaching his students that if you change all of your mistakes and regrets, you'd erase yourself.

Letter from Your New Psychiatrist // Dr. Sonia Patel

Dear Teen Patient,

If you are reading this letter, then your first appointment with me has been scheduled. I look forward to meeting you in person and getting to know you and your circumstances as fully as possible.

I wonder, what is your suffering like? Perhaps your mood is rock bottom. Or is it irritable, worried, enraged, swinging, or shameful? Are your thoughts on overdrive, paranoid, or screaming at you that you're a worthless piece of crap? Are painful memories hijacking you without warning? Are you having sleep difficulties? Are you drinking or drugging? Are you refusing to eat or making yourself throw up? Are your grades slipping or are you terrified of getting less than an A+? Are you getting into fights — verbal or physical? Are you cutting yourself? Wanting to disappear or kill yourself? Or maybe you are suffering in other ways.

I don't know you yet, but I do know that your symptoms of suffering are not a result of psychiatric diagnoses. Did you know that those diagnoses do not actually exist? They are a construct to label clusters of symptoms. Besides offering people the first glimmer of validation of their suffering — and being utilized by health insurance companies to determine payment decisions and by schools to guide student accommodations — psychiatric diagnoses are otherwise mostly useless to suffering individuals.

Let that sink in for a moment.

Now, imagine if after a mere fifty minutes or less of talking with you, I branded you with the psychiatric diagnoses of, let's say, Major Depressive Disorder and Generalized Anxiety Disorder. Not only would my ability to consider other things in your life automatically be limited, but it might be difficult for me to relate to you as a human full of complexities. I might discount things you described that did not fit your "diagnoses" and pay more attention to those things that did. You might leave my office disempowered by the false narrative of being flawed with mental disease.

Let me be clear: you are not flawed with mental disease. Your genes don't code for your symptoms. While genes can predispose people to developing symptoms if environmental interplay encourages it, no single gene on its own has been proven as causative of "psychiatric diagnoses."

There is, however, strong scientific evidence that emotional invalidation from experiences during childhood and teenage years — even without abuse and neglect — causes damage to developing brain structures and functioning, and this damage manifests as symptoms of suffering.

Your symptoms of suffering are a biological response to something external.

Let that sink in for a moment.

Now consider this: as one or more of a myriad of possible emotionally invalidating experiences (such as being bullied, living through family turmoil or parental conflict, being subtly and constantly gaslit, controlled, or belittled by adults or peers, or being shamed or groomed by trusted adults) damages your developing brain, not only do symptoms of suffering appear, but healthy interpersonal attachments are thwarted, your true thoughts and feelings remain elusive, and growing into your authentic self is impossible.

So, when you step into my office and take a seat on the black leather couch across from me, I won't diagnose you. Rather, you and I will begin with a discussion of your symptoms of suffering and your life circumstances. Together, we will take a long, hard look at what is happening and what you are witnessing at home, at school, with your friends, and with all the relevant people and situations in your life. We will unpack how aspects of your relationships and experiences might—with or without intention—be causing you harm and emotional invalidation.

Our work together will not result in you playing the victim to your experiences or blaming anyone. Instead, you will come to understand that your symptoms of suffering and negative patterns of existing in the world did not develop in a void but as a response to the dysfunction in your surrounding system. You will begin to comprehend that since you aren't flawed, healing doesn't fall solely on your shoulders and is a process that involves both you and the system you are growing up in.

Daunting as this may seem, you won't have to go through it alone. I will be with you every step of the way. I will teach you how to identify and distance yourself from your hardwired symptoms of suffering so you can learn how to think, feel, and act as your authentic self. You will learn how to and practice determining and asserting your true thoughts and feelings, setting appropriate boundaries with people and situations, pulling yourself out of past and future tripping back to the moment, rationally responding to interpersonal challenges instead of reacting, and emotionally validating yourself without the need for external reassurance. And that is just the tip of the iceberg.

Eventually, your agency and confidence will bloom, even if the people in your surrounding system refuse to make all of the necessary healing changes we point out to them.

I can't wait to begin guiding you on your healing journey. See you soon.

Best wishes,
Sonia Patel, M.D.

Sonia Patel is a psychiatrist and author of the Morris Award finalist *Rani Patel In Full Effect* and In the Margins Book Award winners *Jaya and Rasa: A Love Story* and *Bloody Seoul*. Her fourth YA novel, *Gita Desai Is Not Here to Shut Up*, will be published September 2024.

Family Portrait in Scars // Kayla Whaley

1. Two inches long, the center of my upper right thigh. Muscle biopsy, age two. The anesthesia didn't work. They carved the chunk out with only Novocaine numbing the skin. I remember screaming. Slightly above and to the right is a freckle, like an eye to the scar's mouth, like a winking face in my leg.

2. A long arc low on my mother's belly. C-section, May 19, 1991, age twenty-six. Three months before my younger sister was due. Mom thought she was constipated right up until her water broke.

3. The length of my spine, curved this way and that. Spinal fusion, fourth grade. Only six days in the hospital. Therapy dogs were coming on the seventh, but the doctors wouldn't let me stay.

4. A starburst of a bruise, my sister's right foot. I misjudged the distance between us in the mirror—closer than they appear. I didn't realize that bump was her foot. My chair, mid-wheel drive: turned on a dime. She didn't scream, but her mouth stretched in the mirror like a surrealist painting, her body lifting upward, as if to loose herself. I froze until she whisper-shouted, "Move!" The bruise lasted months, faded eventually to slight discoloration. Probably a fractured metatarsal, but she never got it checked. On that foot now: a tattoo of the bird-headed man from "Bird-Headed Man with Bison" at Lascoux.

5. Do tattoos count as scars? Do piercings? Does the barely-there line I'm so fond of on the inside of my thumb count if I can't remember its source?

6. Psoriasis across the full terrain of my dad's knuckles. No cure. Insurance stopped covering the cream he used to keep the scales in check. These days he eats cans of tuna for the omega-3 fatty acids, slurping the leftover water straight from the sharp rim; his knuckles are a gentle pink, like the flaky gleam of certain scallop shells.

7. A small, circular burn, right side of my neck. Mole removal, mid-teens, elective. The dermatologist suggested seeing a plastic surgeon to ensure "less of a mark."

8. Two precise trails of small, circular burns along the inside of my sister's left forearm. Cigarette burns, age twenty, self-inflicted. Faded now. Under the emergency room lights, though, fresh and molten. An anchor to hold me inside those white walls instead of letting myself float away.

9. A short-lived scar, which is to say, a contradiction: a diamond-shaped patch of skin scraped off my chest, age twenty-five, self-inflicted. The skin heated as I scratched. Satisfying friction. Satisfying, too, the burst of red in the mirror and the watery film that built up soon after and sooner still congealed to pus. After the infection cleared, a raised scar I'd hoped would fade into a blush-tinted memento but faded instead back to skin.

10. A purple splotch on the back of my sister's right hand. Ironing accident, age twenty-three, running late for work. The restaurant's guests asked about it for months, until the mark matured and turned rich as the wine she served them.

11. An ever-changing array of cuts, scrapes, and pale patches of healed-over skin on Dad's forearms. From cats' claws or dogs' claws, metal edges or metal tools or branches. Sometimes from seemingly nothing at all. The older he gets, the thinner his skin becomes.

12. A lattice of carefully shallow cuts the length of my sister's thighs. The usual instruments, pre-teens to mid-twenties. We were having dinner at Texas Roadhouse when she, eleven, showed us the first one. Pails of whole peanuts sat on every table and shucked shells carpeted the floor. The burgers were thick, peppery, slathered with mayonnaise. The pre-dinner rolls (warm, glazed golden) were served with pats of cinnamon butter, a surprising sweetness. We never ate there again.

13. Third degree burns on Mom's face, left arm, and side. Car crash, age fifteen. Her friend, drunk, hit a telephone pole. Mom wasn't wearing a seat belt. She fell out the passenger-side door and the car rolled on top of her. She was trapped for ten, fifteen minutes. Long enough for her skin and the muscle beneath to burn away where it touched the undercarriage, for gravel to embed in the wounds.

14. To clean her wounds, doctors applied gauze with ointment and—after cementing—ripped both gauze and damaged tissue away. A recurring process. She quickly learned the sound of her doctor's shoes. Whenever she heard the distinctive click-clack on tile, she started screaming.

15. The unknown-to-me ones.

16. The ones unknown to each of our own selves.

17. A sunken area on the inside of Mom's left bicep. Presumably from the crash, like the others. "No," she told me, age twenty-seven. "My nose came from my arm." For months, her arm was attached to her face so the doctors could graft the skin and shape it, like damp clay, into a nose.

18. A notch scooped out of the shell of my right ear. Growth removal. Caused by recurring pressure. Dad scoops a hole from my pillow. Nightly, Mom sweeps my hair away from the sensitive curve. I still sleep with my ear in the hollow, cradled in the protective lack.

Kayla Whaley holds an MFA from the University of Tampa and is former senior editor of Disability in Kidlit. Her work has appeared in anthologies including *Unbroken, Vampires Never Get Old, Game On*, and *Allies*. She is also the author of chapter book series *A to Z Animal Mysteries*.

Slow Burn // Erin Murphy

The day my brother nearly burns down the house, I am sitting on the living room floor.

Correction: It's not a house but an apartment, my father's first since the divorce.

I am playing with Lincoln Logs on the burnt-orange shag carpet, building and rebuilding a perfect house with a green roof.

Correction: I'm not playing; I'm killing time until we're returned to our real home with our real toys and our real parent.

My father is taking a nap in the apartment's only bedroom.

Correction: It's not a nap but his usual stupor, a label for which we won't have for years.

I see the fire out of the corner of my eye.

Correction: What I see first is the shadow puppet of a fire performing on the kitchen wall; mesmerized, I watch for the better part of a minute before investigating its cause.

When I crane my neck around the corner, I see my two-year-old brother waving a brown paper bag that he has dipped in the lit burner of the gas stove. Pretty, he exclaims. Pretty! Pretty!

Correction: He can't pronounce pretty. *He says* pity.

I knock the burning bag from my brother's hand and scream for our father, who bolts from the bedroom and douses the flames.

Correction: Our father doesn't respond until I shake him awake; he extinguishes the fire with a pot of cold, two-day-old coffee. My brother's exclamations soften to a whisper: Pity. Pity. Pity.

No correction necessary.

Erin Murphy is the author or editor of more than a dozen books, most recently Fluent in Blue (Grayson Books). Her work has appeared in The Best of Brevity, Ecotone, The Georgia Review, Rattle, Women's Studies Quarterly, and elsewhere. She is professor of English at Penn State Altoona. www.erin-murphy.com

An Indian in Yoga Class: Finding Imbalance // Rajpreet Heir

Sukhasana
My intent for the day's practice: become more Indian. As an Indian from Indiana who has never been to India, I want to get in touch with my roots, and doing yoga seems like a fun way to do that.

Ommmmmm
As we flutter our eyelids open, Brittany, the instructor, says, "Today we're going to focus on our third chakra, where Ganesh lives and Buddha sometimes visits. Unleash your Kali!" I'm Sikh and don't know my Hindu gods that well, except for a couple lessons from history classes, but I'm not sure Buddha is supposed to be included with them. But what do I know? Brittany is the authority on this stuff. Also, she has Sanskrit tattoos and I don't.

Vinyasa
As everyone raises prayer hands to the ceiling for a sun salutation in time to Major Lazer, Kyle from the front desk sneaks in to photograph the class for the studio's Instagram page, just like the Indians did thousands of years ago. #YouAreEnough #BeHereNow #StrengthGoals #yogaeverygoddamnday #Namaslay #MadRelax #GoodVibes #NamasteAF

Tadasana
"Pick a dristi—I know, such an exotic word," says Brittany. Would the name Kristy be exotic in India? Or Misty? Rice Krispie? We only have distant relatives left in India, but I suppose I could ask my British relatives who go to India more frequently than my American side.

Bakasana
"I'm so happy I got a spot in this class," the woman next to me says as we wait for Brittany to get us blocks. "Brittany discovered yoga in 2009 and brought it to America. She knows everyone in India by name and the color of their aura. And she was asked to star in Slumdog Millionaire but turned it down because the title made it seem like a movie on consumerism." I think about the $300 I paid for a ten-class card. Maybe the classes are expensive because the studio has exceptional instructors?

Ardha Matsyendrasana
As I twist toward the wall, I see a poster for a sari draping class taking place in the studio later that week. I could ask my mom to teach me the next time I'm home, but Brittany probably knows more. Brittany has henna on her hands and a nose piercing, neither of which my mom has.

Virabhadrasana

"Stand strong in this pose, one hand reaching into the future toward Juice Generation, and another reaching back toward the past, Starbucks. Stay in the present and think about how good you look in your Lululemons," Brittany instructs. "Concentration is key here...or karma will not lead us to nirvana."

An interruption

Kyle opens the door and walks down the center of the room. He announces, "Yoga—it's a way of life" then throws clouds of turmeric into the air. People around me raise their hands to it in devotion, swaying side to side on their sitz bones, while other yogis start snorting it off the hardwood floor. #bliss

Setu Bandha Sarvangasana

"Rameshwaria, move your hands closer to the backs of your heels." "My name is actually Rajpreet," I reply. "It's Rameshwaria since I knew a Rameshwaria once." "But my name is Rajpreet." "No."

Shavasana

Brittany explains this is the hardest pose and it really does feel like it. I don't feel relaxed, in fact, I feel more stressed than when I arrived. A white woman is teaching me about yoga, an ancient Indian practice, and she thinks she's an expert on Indian culture too, but I don't know exactly which ways I can be mad because I don't know enough about India or yoga myself, partly because I feel a pressure to assimilate. But darn it if Brittany's playlist isn't fun.

Namaste

(The cultural appropriation in me bows to the Indian in you.)

Putting away mats

"What other instructors would you recommend?" I ask Brittany. "Katie, Jenny, Julie, Courtney, Zoey, Christy, Mary, Lucy, Hayley Ashley, Natalie, Lindsey, Kaylee, Lizzy, and Audrey are amaze."

Exit

I follow the trail of organic quinoa down the hall to the door and leave feeling very Indian American.

Rajpreet Heir received her B.A. in English Writing from DePauw University and her M.F.A. in Creative Nonfiction from George Mason University. An assistant professor of creative nonfiction at Ithaca College, she now lives in Ithaca, New York. Rajpreet has work in *The Atlantic, The Washington Post, The New York Times, Teen Vogue, Brevity, The Normal School,* and others.

The Heroine // Rachel Toalson

Someone once told her she could do **anything**.

She had no idea what it meant. **Anything** was so large and ambiguous and limitless; surely she couldn't do *anything*. There were rules to her world. Don't talk too loud. Don't be too bossy. Remember to smile. Be happy with what you have, and don't want more. Stay in your place. Dress modestly. Don't act like a tease. Don't go anywhere alone. Curb your ambition, or at least don't talk about it.

There were so many rules she couldn't remember them all. Don't be dependent but also don't be too independent. Love your job but also don't love your job too much. Do your best but also don't *be the best*. Speak up but also shut the hell up.

How could she do **anything** when she lived with so many contradictions? She could hardly get dressed every day without an existential crisis — did this shirt show too much skin, did these pants cling too tightly to her ass, was she walking around as a breathing distraction *who knows the answers who can bear the questions*

It took her years to finally understand she got to define **anything**, not the world.

Rachel Toalson is the author of *The Colors of the Rain, The Woods, The First Magnificent Summer*, and *Something Maybe Magnificent* (Simon & Schuster, 2024). Her poetry has been published in print magazines and literary journals around the world. She lives in San Antonio, Texas, with her husband and six sons.

Crabby Hermits and Simone Biles: Using Satire and Experimental Forms // Carlos Greaves

Simone Biles had just withdrawn from the women's gymnastics team event at the Tokyo Olympics, and reading Piers Morgan's tweet made my blood boil.

"Are 'mental health issues' now the go-to excuse for any poor performance in elite sport? What a joke."

How someone with zero experience competing in elite sports — let alone Olympic gymnastics — could say something so heartless and ignorant about an athlete's struggles was baffling to me. So, as a satirist, I did what I normally do when I read something that makes me incandescently angry — I tried to write something funny about it.

Short humor pieces published in places like *McSweeney's* and *The New Yorker* often use an existing form as a template, anything from BINGO, to math problems, to a spoof of the *New York Times'* "Connections" game.

This writing technique is called a hermit crab essay, and here is everything you need to know about what hermit crab essays are and how to write one

FAQ About Hermit Crab Essays

What is a hermit crab essay?

A hermit crab essay is one in which the writer uses an existing form such as a letter, a quiz, or a product review, as a structure for their writing.

What are some examples of hermit crab essays?

- Brenda Miller's rejection letters essay, "We Regret to Inform You"

- Samantha Irby's recipe essay, "an instagram frittata"

- "Thanksgiving Rider" by Simon Rich

Is this FAQ an example of a hermit crab essay?

Yes, how very astute of you. But was that actually a question, or are you one of those people who likes to ask questions they know the answer to in order to show off how smart they are?

How do you choose what form to use for your hermit crab essay?

I'm so glad you asked. Often, the form conveys something about the author or the characters. Samantha Irby's recipe essay, for example, tells us about her complicated relationship with food. In the case of "Thanksgiving Rider," the use of legalese reveals the ways in which the relationship between the mother and daughter feels contractual and carefully negotiated.

Is it called a hermit crab essay because the author is adopting a "shell" for their essay much like a hermit crab?

No, it's because writers are all crabby hermits. Yes, of course that's why it's called a hermit crab essay. But, again, I'm pretty sure you asked this question already knowing the answer, you obnoxious little teacher's pet, you.

What are some benefits of hermit crab essays?

- Constraints are a great way to combat writer's block. Having a specific form to work off of can help eliminate the paralysis of choice when tackling a topic.

- Form can add a layer of humor as well as get the author's point of view across more effectively.

- Hermit crab essays are also a great way to structure essays about hermit crab essays because they provide a concrete example of a hermit crab essay while allowing the author to insert running jokes that make the essay more fun to read.

Do hermit crab essays always have to include meta humor?

No, that's just a thing I enjoy doing.

As I was brainstorming ways to satirize Piers Morgan's tweet, I thought about how unqualified he was to weigh in on Biles' decision to withdraw. That got me thinking: is *anyone* qualified to criticize the greatest gymnast of all time? That question inspired my

43

piece, Are You Allowed to Criticize Simone Biles?: A Decision Tree, which uses a flowchart to guide the reader through questions like "Are you a gymnast? Yes or No?" and "Did you win four gold medals in women's gymnastics at the 2016 Olympic Games in Rio de Janeiro? Yes or No?" Gradually, as the reader follows the flowchart, it becomes clear that the only person allowed to criticize Simone Biles is Simone Biles.

A few days after the piece was published, a friend texted me, "Check out Simone's Twitter page!" There, under the "likes" section, was a link to my piece. That my piece about Simone Biles, borne out of second-hand frustration and written by a stranger half a world away, was able to reach Biles herself was empowering as a writer. And look, I'm not saying my piece was the reason Simone was able to bounce back so quickly and win a bronze medal in the balance beam. But I'm also not *not* saying that (I'm kidding, she bounced back so quickly because she's Simone freaking Biles). Still, maybe an essay with the right form can be just the thing to reach someone struggling to find a form of their own.

Carlos Greaves is an Afro-Latino engineer, writer, and filmmaker. His writing can be found in *The New Yorker*, *NPR*, *McSweeney's*, and his Substack newsletter, *Shades of Greaves*. His debut book, *Spoilers: Essays That Might Ruin Your Favorite Hollywood Movies* is available wherever you get your books.

Zilelian from Zile // Aida Zilelian

'Es Mari Zilelyan em. From Turkiye, Amasya. Maybe you and me cosins. No good inglis. Sorry.'

I received this message last year on Facebook. The woman in the profile looked to be in her mid-seventies and lived in California. She sent me long messages, at first in Turkish, explaining that her father was born in the town of Zile and she had been searching for years to find her father's missing brother, her uncle Garabed. He had disappeared during the Genocide. Could it be we're related? she asked.

My name is Aida Zilelian. My father Harutiun immigrated to Sunnyside, Queens in the early 60's with his sister Marie, my grandmother Shaké and my grandfather Garabed. Orphaned during the Genocide, he had led a difficult life; he had been arrested and arrested as an adolescent for killing a Turk, he had lived under Romania's communist regime selling goods on the black market and was imprisoned several times, and inevitably, moved to America in his fifties, dying as a foreigner, his native country a foreign place in his memory.

It was only last year, after calling my aunt, that I came to understand the origin of my last name. Zile, a city and district of the Tokat Province in Turkey, where my grandfather was born. It was where my grandfather Garabed's family was burned to death during the Genocide, from where my grandfather had escaped at six years old and managed to live despite the odds. There is very little else I know about him; he had a violent temper and died of a heart attack.

As a child, I grew up surrounded by my mother's family, a boisterous and stubborn clan of Lebanese-Armenians, quick-witted and hilarious. The maternal side of my family is strewn throughout California and Rhode Island. My mother told us stories about her cousins in Beirut, their antics and close-knit existence where they lived among an enclave of Armenians before immigrating to America. Throughout the years, my mother's family seemed to multiply. We'd hear a name for the first time – her cousin Boghos who lived in Paris, her cousin Peggy who had recently gotten divorced – whether first or second or twice removed (whatever that means, really) my mother's bloodline was extensive. Who are these people? my sisters and I would ask. This is the first we're hearing their names. My mother would wave us off, That's nothing, she would say. That's just from your grandmother's side.

I think now about my father, being raised by his taciturn father and his compliant mother, whose relatives had also perished during the Genocide. He could not name an aunt or uncle, he heard no amusing anecdotes assuring him of his roots, his family's legacy. Though he never spoke of his sense of alienation he revived the memory of my grandfather Garabed again and again, boasting of his bravery in Romania when he distributed illegal goods to his Armenian friends and neighbors at the risk of being caught. We learned of how he had survived after watching his family tied at the wrists, a mortifying link that bound them before they were set on fire, how he had run and hid from one village to the next before finding himself in France somehow.

If what Mari Zilelyan said was true, she would be my father's first cousin. Her father would have been my great-uncle. Shortly after hearing from Mari, I received a message from her daughter and we began communicating with an ease that assumed a long-lost friendship, as if the years had carelessly slipped away. She wanted us to take a DNA test. She, more than I, was confident that we were related. "Second cousins," she said. "I can tell just from talking to you. We're definitely related."

I didn't dare believe it. The disappointment would be too great. Had my father been alive, I would have been tempted to tell him about my correspondence. When the testing kit arrived I let it sit on the dining room table for weeks before bothering to open the box. I probably would have thrown it away if I had not committed to taking it.

I told my Uncle Hagop about Mari, knowing he would be especially interested because he personally knew Armenians from his community who had reunited with their families decades after the Genocide. He sent me newspaper articles. I read over each reluctantly, a small hope blooming. A brother and sister find one another fifty years after being separated, a refugee orphan who grows up in Egypt is found by her sister's family, both siblings in their seventies. Did the fortune of finding one another eclipse all the lost years? It seemed a miracle, nonetheless.

"Did you get your results yet? I'm not seeing your name," Mari's daughter wrote, fraught with undertones of disappointment. "I have matches, but I already know those relatives." I assured her that I hadn't received anything yet. "I'm going to be shocked if we're not related," she said. By that point, she and I had continued our communication through texting and video chatting. I had met her teenage sons and spoken to them, learned about her amicable divorce. "My mom is going to want to speak to you and tell you all about your grandfather's family. We all live miles away from each other. You can fly out with your family!" was her last message.

That very day I received the email with my DNA results. I fumbled through the website, finally clicking on the 'common ancestors' icon, a short queue of names appearing. I scrolled too quickly, and then began at the top of the list, reading through each name slower than necessary. Slow enough to come to grips with the fact that Mari and I were not blood relatives. I consoled myself with the fact that I hadn't shared my correspondence with Mari and her daughter with anyone other than my husband and my uncle, that I didn't have to deliver the disappointing news to anyone, really. It was just me. As if I mattered little. The photographs she could have shown me of relatives bearing resemblance to my father's small family. The story of how they had survived, despite my grandfather's grim recollection of them being murdered. Where they had settled, thrived. The family tree that would blossom, its limbs extending magically like an unfurling seed.

I looked at a photograph of my father and his sister, my grandparents. A black and white picture of them sitting on a large rock, smiling faintly, squinting in the sunlight. My father is barely twenty years old as he sits next to my grandfather Garabed, an aged version of what my father will grow to resemble in the passing years. My grandfather will live only a few short years after the photo is taken.

It would be in my best interest to find a decorative bow and wrap what I have written here with clumsy sentiment or perhaps unveil some small triumph, a revelation. I have none. What I am left with is how singular I feel, like so many others, I imagine. I think of my grandfather and the small city of Zile, his large family extinguished and how he managed to live despite the circumstances. He prospered and married, had children. And that I am still here.

Aida Zilelian is a first generation American-Armenian writer, educator and storyteller from Queens, NY. She is the author of *The Legacy of Lost Things* (2015, Bleeding Heart Publications) which was the recipient of the 2014 Tololyan Literary Award. Aida's most recently completed novel, *All the Ways We Lied* (Keylight Books/Turner Bookstore).

Just
fiction

love land world futures being

Hot Lunch Petition // Aimee Parkison

A hungry kindergartner came to the cafeteria worker, Macy Dolan, crying because she couldn't pay for her school lunch. Macy did what any cafeteria worker with a heart would do. She drove to the kindergartner's house and used a frozen pepperoni pizza to beat up the kindergartner's mother, who claimed the child should eat for free.

Unfortunately, the elementary school where Macy was employed has a policy against giving students free food. According to protocol, the situation is handled in this manner: The first three times a student is unable to pay, the lunch is taken to the bathroom by a cafeteria worker and flushed down the toilet before the child's eyes. The fourth time, the school provides a hat shaped like a cheese sandwich and milk.

Macy had seen the ridicule these children endure when their peers witness them wearing that cheese on a bun. She also saw these children's energy wane because they weren't being nutritionally sustained by flushed lunches. But what really bothered her was the way soggy pizzas began backing up toilets in the school restrooms. The melted cheese on the toilet rims, along with the pepperoni and tomato sauce swirling, pushed her too far.

Near cafeteria trash cans overflowing with squandered food, poor children huffed fumes of hot lunches the rich kids threw away. Soon, even rich kids began huffing hot lunches from the trash as they learned the fumes could get them high.

Unfortunately, we live in a country where rich kids are "kids" and poor kids are not "kids" but "children." We live in a country where food is flushed away by adults or trashed in stinking heaps by rich kids while poor children go hungry. Just to get by, poor children have to invent new ways for rich kids to get high. But everyone, rich or poor, has one thing in common, and that is the need for toilets.

That is why Macy Dolan uses food as a weapon, wielding a frozen pizza at the faces of the parents of hungry children. Now that she has been fired, she is calling on the School District to reinstate her for saving toilets sacrificed to childhood hunger.

A person who cares this much about toilets belongs in our schools.

Aimee Parkison has published eight books and won FC2's Catherine Doctorow Innovative Fiction Prize and *North American Review*'s Kurt Vonnegut Prize. She is Professor of Fiction Writing at OSU. Her work has appeared in *North American Review*, *Puerto Del Sol*, *Five Points*, and *Best Small Fictions*. www.aimeeparkison.com

The Blue Jay // Tamara Belko

The Blue Jay was dead. Its mangled carcass coughed up on the front lawn, a red ribboned present from our orange tabby. Or maybe it was an omen. In any case, it didn't matter because I was late. Very late. The dead bird would have to remain where it met its demise until after school when I could give it a proper burial next to the deceased bunnies and chipmunks that was our animal cemetery.

My day would sink into more gloom as the sky opens and rain splashes my windshield on my short drive to school. Puddles. Everywhere. Squeaky, slippery hallways. A skinny kid with shaggy hair and bad acne goes down and, of course, everyone laughs because, yeah, that's funny. The laughter adds to my gloom. That was not remotely funny.

I help the kid pick up his scattered books. We avoid eye contact. He mumbles, "thank you."

Someone snickers, "Stupid freshman."

I trudge to my first class, slump into my seat and find myself thinking about the dead bird on my front lawn. Again. I find myself thinking about everything we've buried: family, sadness, guilt.

Will my little brother see the corpse and cry? I usually dispose of the bodies before he spots them. Not that he doesn't know they are buried in our backyard. Not that he doesn't help make stick crosses. It's just that he imagines them whole, in peaceful repose, crossing into animal heaven. He doesn't see them broken, entrails strewn across the yard. My stomach sours at the thought. I hope he doesn't see. Hope he doesn't feel the sinking sadness. I'll tell him it is all part of life. The tabby is a natural predator. Don't hold this death against our cat. It's the natural order of things. Natural order. Then how to explain death that subverts that order? Illness that strikes children, like the neighbor's grandson who suffered his entire life before succumbing to cancer.

My thoughts are interrupted by the principal's voice on the PA saying there is a lockdown drill. Silently, we slip to the dark recesses of the room. Make ourselves small, pretend that we would survive an armed gunman rampaging through our halls. As the minutes tick by, I consider how we would really respond if there were an actual active shooter. Would we be huddled, obediently, in silence? Or would we be whimpering? Or screaming? Would the shooter pierce our door with bullets, break the glass pane? Shoot us all? Or would he continue down the hall to discover our friends hiding in other classrooms. They said most victims of gunshot wounds die from blood loss. I imagine blood, ribbons of blood.

But this is a drill. A drill.

"This concludes our lockdown drill. Please remain in your rooms until your doors are unlocked." Mr. Murphy's voice crackles over the PA.

I try to shake the morbid thoughts from my head. But the thoughts linger all day. Dead BlueJays, tiny stick crosses peppered across our lawn, dead children, blood soaking the floor.

When I get home, the rain has finally stopped. At least, the wet earth will yield easily. I pull the car into the garage, retrieve the shovel and head to the front yard, to the Blue Jay, intending to give the bird a proper burial.

But the bird is gone.

Tamara Belko is a reader, writer and teacher. As a middle school English teacher and Power of the Pen Creative writing coach, Tamara has spent her career sharing her passion for reading, writing and poetry with her students. Tamara is the author of young adult verse novel *Perchance to Dream.*

The Reason // Val Howlett

Before I almost died, I always felt agitated, like there was something jittery in my chest and head. I used to let it out by talking, making jokes, tearing people down. But after, I got that feeling replaced by this calm that's nice, but only for me. No one else can handle it. My friends call me "Surfer Brian" now, even though I play baseball. I can't go a day without my mom or stepdad or my sister saying "What's with you?" My sister literally booed me the other day, after she came downstairs in this low-cut outfit and way too much makeup and mom started giving her hell and they all looked at me to say something, but all I said was, "What? If you feel good that's what matters."

I thought Paige liked this me, Surfer Brian or whatever you want to call the me that almost died. But now I'm worried she only likes me because of my near-death experience.

Paige is in my English class, so she knew about it. Our teacher singled me out one day and made me read my personal essay aloud, which was about dying and what I saw after. That huge room, from above. The tunnel and the light. And then Miss let the class debate whether my brain made it up. They were like my family—more people wanted to question it than believed me. I got arguments like, "You took pills, right? You drank and took pills? How do you know you weren't hallucinating?" and "Did you know brains hallucinate when they're deprived of oxygen?" I tried to tell them how clear it was, not like drugs at all. Paige didn't say anything.

But wasn't it just a few days later that she hit on me? The way she walked clear across the room and asked me if I wanted her candy bar because it had hazelnuts and she was allergic—like there was no one near her own desk.

Paige had a reputation for being intense. Following her online confirmed it—her posts were all paranormal this and hauntings that. Past Me would've run the other way.

But I liked that she signaled at me so clear, that she knew what she wanted. I think people pass her over because she talks about invisible stuff while staring right into their eyes. But I think, or I thought, that with my jitteriness gone, I could see too much of everyone else. I could tell what they were trying for when they talked, which is usually so different from what they say, and it's a lot—like two songs playing at the same time. Paige's needs pretty much matched how she talked.

I thought. But she was holding something back, at first. Because it took a couple weeks of texting before she mentioned my death. It made sense with our conversation—I was talking about my family, about how I'd been so much more chill after that night, nicer, yet they seemed more mad at me than ever. She'd messaged, "You know, it's actually really common for people who had NDEs to have trouble with their loved ones."

She said NDEs meant near-death experiences, that she'd heard a podcast about them. I was moved by that.

But then she kept bringing it up. She said, "Tell me what you saw after you died" right after we hooked up the first time. We were lying together in my sister's car.

I told her. Even though she'd already heard my paper. I told her because she was fearless and at the same time, soft.

I told her things I'd never written, too, like how the light wasn't just visual—it was a feeling. It moved through me. I felt it filling my body, dissolving the jitteriness, opening me up to more.

She asked, "Did you see anything else?"

I should've known then. Or when she texted me questions after. Did I see any other people who died? Was I given a message?

It happened again this morning, on a real date that I set up and everything. I'd heard it was going to weirdly warm for February, so I searched for a pretty place and found a trail in Fairview. She met me there in a cute sweater instead of her normal hoodie, sitting on the grass all prepared with a backpack full of bottled water and snacks.

But we hadn't gone five minutes down the path before she said, "Don't you think there's a reason why you came back to life?"

I must've got a look on my face because she stopped and said, "What? Why don't you want to tell me?"

We fought. I told her to stop trying to be my therapist. I called her jealous. I felt like I used to, like something was buzzing around inside me.

She stood blocking the path like a security guard, like a wronged TV girlfriend, and yelled that I had to be keeping something from her—that I couldn't travel so far out of this life and bring back nothing. Hadn't I seen anybody, like a grandparent who passed, or Becks from elementary school? "Remember?" she said. "The girl who died of esophageal cancer in fifth grade?" The need was rocketing off her, and I was so thrown that she had an agenda, a name. That she hadn't really heard me. She thought the biggest thing that had ever happened to me wasn't enough.

I pushed past her, walked deeper down the trail. I don't know if she tried to follow. She claimed there had to be a reason I was here, but she wanted it to be *her* reason. She was missing the point. I had found a pretty place. Green and flowers were budding on trees. Baseball season hadn't started yet and it was Saturday morning. We had a whole open day ahead of us. The reason was right here.

Val Howlett is a folktale lover, curious researcher, and bookish florist. Their fiction has appeared in *Lunch Ticket*, *Hunger Mountain*, and two anthologies: *Ab(solutely) Normal: Short Stories That Smash Mental Health Stereotypes* and *We Mostly Come Out at Night: 15 Queer Tales of Monsters, Angels & Other Creatures*.

This Story is Against Resilience, Supports Screaming As Needed // Jen Ferguson

A girl wearing a frilly pink apron bursts out of the screen door the kitchen staff keep open for air-flow even in winter. She kicks at a plastic milkcrate, sending it barreling across the alley into the side of that black vat where used oil gets stored until a big truck comes to suck it all up.

The girl pauses. Then screams. Her breath fogs the air.

The scream is bitter, rough. The kind that will hurt later.

The girl is *fine* with that.

Retrieving the milkcrate, flipping it, she sits, tries to extract a lone cigarette lodged in her pocket. The girl is out of patience—she's just *sick* of being patient, of those well-meaning people calling her *resilient*. Every day, but especially *today*.

When the cigarette comes free, it breaks in half. There's too much *pressure*.

The girl drops the pieces at her feet.

She *stews*. But doesn't explode again. Enough of that.

Behind her, the screen door creaks open. "There you are, Cams. None of those jokers you work with said you were on break."

The other girl is taller. Not a girl really. Not anymore. Now that she's grown, her sister's ditched the red eyeliner she used to wear *all day long*. The memorial tat, the one with the sweetgrass braid, is covered by a puffy neon orange coat, like she's going off hunting.

Like she doesn't want to end up *hunted*.

"Well, you found me," Cami huffs, remembering why she stormed out: *that* word. Like it's a compliment, not another burden. Like survival is *enough*.

"Don't tell me that's yours?" her sister asks, all adjacent-to-sanctimonious like she didn't smoke those clove cigarettes even after *the good old* government turned them contraband.

"You've got exactly no cred here, eh, Tyler?"

"You're right, I don't. Who's buying for you anyhow? Who do I have to beat up?"

Cami loves being right. But it's not *enough*. "Thought you weren't doing *that* anymore?"

"I'm not. But you know I'd resurrect anytime, for you, eh?"

Cami just nods. She *knows*.

"So, yeah, food tonight? Jaxon's home from the rigs. Wants to have family dinner. Sent me out to buy steaks. We'll do up corn, maybe asparagus, long as it's not stringy and sad."

"It's not *family* dinner." Cami bites the inside of her cheek. "Jaxon's not family."

"You're in that kind of mood today. Got it. I'll just tell our stepdad, who shows up for us, constantly — "

" — when he's home!"

" — when he's not working! Yeah, I'll tell him that."

The sisters fall quiet. A truck in the parking lot struggles to turn over. Noise from the kitchen filters between them.

When they speak, it's at the same time.

"Don't. I'm only talking."

"Cams, I have news." A small white envelope emerges from a puffy orange jacket pocket. The envelope's been crushed and folded and unfolded. "I was gonna save this for dinner but... I applied. I got in."

Suddenly, Cami's relieved. It tastes like the diner's wintergreen mints. All she says, flat, is: "Edmonton's not *that* far."

"Actually, this one's from Tkaronto." Tyler digs into her pocket again. "And this one's from Newfoundland. And I have email yesses from UBC, McMaster, McGill. Calgary even. All of them coming through with that scholarship money."

"Yeah?"

It's not articulate. But it *is* enough.

Tyler half-smiles. "Edmonton did too, in case you're worried I'm leaving."

Cami rolls her eyes, says it all serious: "Go far away, eh."

In the cold, the sisters' laughter turns exhaled air from a gas into a liquid — that's the science, Cami *knows*, but to her, it's also this tiny, needed *magic*.

"So family dinner tonight?"

"Dinner's good."

A mother's *death anniversary*. The sister who *needs* to leave *this place*. The stepdad a girl might crap on because he's the one who's still around and you can't crap on your dead mom, but your stepdad's fair game *because* he works hard, *loves harder*. All that can exist in the same moment. But so can breath turned into laughter turned magic, breath that makes anger, even this *lingering* anger, visible.

And sometimes — it's truth — a girl needs to step outside into the cold and do a good scream.

Jen Ferguson is Métis with ancestral ties to the Red River and white, an activist, a feminist, an auntie, and an accomplice armed with a PhD. She is the award-winning (and award-losing!) author of *The Summer of Bitter and Sweet*, *Those Pink Mountain Nights* and *A Constellation of Minor Bears*.

Spontaneous Combustion // Kristin Bartley Lenz

They call it a stitch, but it feels like my ribcage is splintering. Still, I run and run, chased by cleats scraping my Achilles. I've already signaled for a sub. My teammates amplify my plea, but Coach is a bellowing bull. "I'm counting on you!"
I count ten girls on the bench who never get to play.
My lungs scorch, I gasp and gag. Bitter bile rises, my white uniform a canvas for the eruption of my sour heart.

***

High school soccer practice is from 4-6pm, but Coach never stops before 6:25. Our parents' SUVs purr in the parking lot, beasts spewing sulfur. We race to gather the cones, herd the balls, drag the nets. We slap sweaty hands, chug plastic polluted water, unwind tape from stressed ankles. We waddle off the field, weighted with two backpacks and two hours of homework.

Back at my house, I eat, shower, and bury my nose deep in my dog's neck. My books and binders are a tower destined to topple. Our coach's parting words every evening: "Remember ladies, prioritize sleep, take care of your bodies."

***

At school, my counselor asks me to rate my stress level, one to ten. How do you rank an ocean's waves ebbing and flowing, receding and rising, tugged by the power of the moon?
"Volunteer hours?"
She's reading from a checklist.
"What are you passionate about?"
I don't tell her that I wrote a poem. About the magnolia tree outside my bedroom window and the petals that feel as smooth as the inside of a seashell.
I don't tell her that I paint my thirteen-year-old brother's fingernails a different color of the rainbow at his request, and how he chips them all bare before morning.
I don't tell her how I sniff peppermint oil before exams, sip ginger tea before games, dab lavender behind my ears to help me sink into sleep past midnight.

I think about telling her about my job washing dogs at the Pet Parlor down the street. How I murmur soothing words as my hands lather shampoo, the smell of wet fur in my nostrils.
I part my lips to speak, but her eyes skitter to her chiming phone. "Find your passion; it will give you purpose," she says, her finger swiping the screen.

***

My mom says I talked in my sleep again, but my words were garbled. I remember my dream, the rapid river that flooded my lungs and drowned my voice. I choked on a fish.

At church on Sunday morning, I exchange a sleepy sideways glance with my brother. Our phones are in the car; an itch we cannot reach. Afterwards, I have seventy-eight messages from my AP Chemistry group chat, an afternoon shift at the Pet Parlor, and an evening of babysitting, but Mom insists we go out for brunch because "I hardly see you."

At the restaurant, my English teacher balances a platter of pancakes two tables over. Her hair is pulled back into two low ponytails.
"She looks twelve," my mom says.
I'm thirty-years-old, but I can't buy a house, my teacher once told us. Her student loans loom as large as a mortgage.
"Liberal arts," my stepdad snorts.

I think about how to keep my Pet Parlor job this summer. The weeks are already scheduled with SAT tutoring, soccer camps, and college visits. Mom expects me to earn a scholarship.
My brother tosses his bangs out of his eyes and drums his hands on the table. He's kept the nail polish on each of his middle fingers. One is blue, one is pink.
"You need a haircut," our stepdad tells him.

Cold air blasts from the vent above our table. I rub my arms and shiver. My mom pulls at the neckline of her blouse and fans herself with her napkin. My stepdad manspreads and snaps his fingers at our waitress, orders more coffee.

I close my eyes and scratch Fuel + O2 → CO2 + H2O across the inside of my eyelids.

If our teenage brains are so undeveloped, why are we able to see the bigger picture, while the adults only see what they want in the moment?

My brother kicks me under the table and tips his head toward the door.

I push my chair back and rise. "We'll wait outside," I tell our parents.

My brother and I bump shoulders on our way out. He holds the door open, and I squint into the sunlight. The warm air feels like a hug.

Kristin Bartley Lenz is a writer and social worker in metro Detroit. Her young adult novel, *The Art of Holding On and Letting Go*, was a Junior Library Guild Selection and a Great Lakes Great Books Award honor book. You can find more of her writing at www.kristinbartleylenz.com.

Her Story // Padma Venkatraman

1

We shoaled into the cafeteria together. We knew who the sharks were, and how to avoid them; we knew exactly where they basked in the afternoon sunshine, waiting to sink their teeth into some poor fish's flesh. We grabbed trays and plastic packets of ketchup and bruised green apples. We watched the lunch-lady fling clumps of brown gravy on scoops of mashed potatoes. Our plates filled, we flitted away to the table in the far corner like fish schooling in a hidden grotto where they're safe to indulge in their own small feeding frenzy.

We knew there was safety in numbers, the three of us. We'd played together and laughed together since second grade. We'd stood side by side for hours to sell girl scout cookies. We'd run against each other at cross country meets. Sure, we'd squabble every now and then – but we knew we belonged to the same species, although our families were so different: Katrice, whose doctor parents came from Eritreya; Laurel, whose dad is a pastor and whose family has lived here for who knows how long; and me, Sandhya who prefers to go by Sandy, because it blends in and it matches my beige skin, which I inherited half from my history-professor mom who came to the States with her parents when she was five, and half from my father's Irish ancestors who probably immigrated during the potato famine.

I saw the new girl at the end of the lunch-line that curled like a scraggly piece of seaweed drying on the beach. It wasn't just the baggy, brightly colored salwar kameez she was wearing that made her stick out so badly; it was also the coconut-oil scent (stronger, I felt sure, than the stale cheese odor that permeated the cafeteria) wafting off her gleaming black hair, which she wore in a tight braid; and, most of all, the bright red bindi on her forehead, exactly like the one my mother insists I paint between my eyebrows on the rare occasions when we visit the temple.

We all saw her eyes dart to our table in the lunchroom. I know we all did, because at once, the three of us fell silent.

We had space for her at our table. We knew she could see that we had space. But we met one another's eyes, not hers, and we stiffened like criminals in the shadows trying to escape her searchlight gaze, until we sensed her gaze had passed over us. Then, our relief tumbled into mindless chatter, mixing easily with the clatter of the not-so-silverware, the clickety-clack of plastic, the thudding trays, the shouts of laughter and echoing waves of noise.

At the dim edge of our horizon, she was visible, sitting alone at a table by the window, bathed in a golden rectangle of sunshine.

2

Her name was Vaishali – an old fashioned Indian name that Mr. Goldberg stumbled over and mispronounced when she walked into his class, later that afternoon.

We were already at our desks, and she gave me a half-wave as she slipped into the seat next to mine. I stared at my desk, pretending I hadn't seen her hesitant hand.

But I couldn't ignore the reason I was avoiding her. For years and years, I'd tried to be as unnoticeable, ordinary, insipid as I could be; and here, suddenly, came this new girl, looking like my grandmother might have done when she was fresh off the boat. She was everything I should have embraced, but also everything I was frightened to love inside me – personified, standing outside me.

3

By the end of her first week, it was easy for us to pretend she didn't exist. We might have forgotten about her altogether and not needed to pretend at all, if it hadn't been for the way the sharks homed in on her.

We didn't snigger when Marlene called her Sasquatch, but we didn't tell her to knock it off, either. When Jacques, leader of the cool gang, walked past her table and threw a handful of bacon bits over her rice, we looked at each other and then looked away.

Self-preservation is an instinct, just as hard to suppress as a shark's thirst for blood.

It was as if we'd made a silent pact, the three of us. We let her eat alone. We let her sit alone. We let her walk alone. We were close-knit friends, and we were happy in our friendship and we didn't need anyone else, after all.

Vaishali became as silent as a storm-tossed bark, and with each new battering, she grew calmer and wiser in a way that won my deepest respect. I did admire her strength – but so secretly that I didn't even admit it to Laurel or Katrice, because the more Vaishali endured, the brighter cowardice grew in my heart. I could feel my fear, shivering like sunlight on the scales of a fish.

4

Mr. Goldberg was a phenomenal history teacher. He had the gift of getting our attention without needing to work for it. We listened to him recount the horrors of the Holocaust, the genocide of our indigenous people, the evils of enslavement and the continuation of those evils, through the Jim Crow era. We read about non-violence connections between Reverend Doctor Martin Luther King Junior and Mahatma Gandhi - whom Vaishali always referred to as Gandhi-ji. We wrote long essays, we debated ideas, we learned to speak out in the classroom.

We thought we learned a great deal.

5

In June, when school was almost over, I noticed that Vaishali had missed a history lesson. We commented on her absence when, at lunchtime, we noticed she wasn't at her usual table.

Maybe she's ill? Laurel said.

Or, maybe her family's moved? Katrice suggested.

Except why would anyone's family move so suddenly, so close to the end of the school year, and that too after joining our school in the middle of that school year?

Or maybe she's away somewhere nice with her family or something, Katrice continued, vaguely. I didn't think Vaishali dressed or behaved like her family had the means to go anywhere nice, but it felt rude to say so, or even think that.

Maybe, I agreed.

We were sure she'd be back, in a day or two.

But three days went by and Vaishali was still nowhere to be seen.

6

They made a great big announcement about what had happened to Vaishali. The bullying had escalated and turned violent.

Jacques and his friends had waited for her after school one day. They might have – who knows what they might have done? All they said was she'd had the presence of mind to call 911 and Jacques and his buddies had been caught on a school security camera. He and his gang were facing suspension – maybe more.

According to our principal, the school would be starting a whole new anti-bullying training program next year. They said they took it seriously, and it must never happen again at our school.

I feel kind of bad, Katrice added.

Not like it was our fault, Laurel said.

For a moment a question hung, unspoken in the air. What if we'd tried to make a place for her at our table?

Then, we shrugged the question away.

7

We didn't talk about Vaishali again. Why would we? The three of us hardly knew her.

I don't think of her often. But every once in a while, I catch myself glancing at the sunlit spot where Vaishali would always sit at lunchtime, silent as a shadow.

Shadows are strange things. We nearly never notice them, but we can never detach ourselves from them. They creep along behind us, lurking in wait for those brief moments when, unexpectedly, the light shifts and they leap ahead of us, forcing us to acknowledge their existence.

Padma Venkatraman's novels *The Bridge Home, Born Behind Bars, A Time to Dance, Island's End* and *Climbing the Stairs,* have secured over 20 starred reviews, won multiple awards and sold > 250,000 copies. Visit www.padmavenkatraman.com to read more about oceanographer-turned-author Dr. Venkatraman and contact https://theauthorvillage.com/presenters/padma-venkatraman/ to arrange a visit.

Get Ready With Me // Taylor Byas

Although her parents had been hinting at the ridiculousness of her morning routine for years now, nothing could stop Aliyah. She was up three hours before the 7:20 bell at school, patting expensive serums and creams into her glistening skin. The few times her mother would come to wake her, she was already up, holding a handheld fan to dry a face mask more quickly or resting against her headboard with two slimy, gold crescents beneath her eyes.

"What do those even *do*?" her mother asked once, tracing half-circles under her own eyes with an index finger. Aliyah answered without opening her eyes, careful not to move her mouth too much and disturb the patches.

"Keeps me pretty, ma." Aliyah heard her mother hesitate in her doorway for a few more moments, saying nothing. Then, when she heard the soft click of her bedroom door, she slipped out of bed and into the bathroom to start on her makeup.

Every paycheck Aliyah earned from her weekend barista gig went to skincare products or high-end foundations, concealers, primers. She no longer listened to music as she primped and prepped but filled the bathroom with the latest beauty influencer's voice. Before her school days even began, she was a student of the cat eye, the cut crease, the perfect contour style for her oval-shaped face. There were 15 minutes scheduled into the morning, right after straightening her tightly-curled hair, just to admire the finished look. In these minutes, her anxiety buzzed the loudest, a faint humming between her ears that only quieted when her focus was elsewhere.

On the morning bus, the looks and whispers as Aliyah pressed towards the back had long stopped. Her classmates were used to the makeup now, and every now and then she even got a compliment from one of the freshman girls who just started experimenting with makeup herself. And yet, when she arrived at her typical seat towards the back, Aliyah always sat alone.

Whenever her parents asked her about her sudden interest in makeup—"interest" being the gentlest way they could rephrase "obsession"—Aliyah insisted that it was a way for her to connect with the popular girls in her grade. She reassured her mother that it was working, that the head of the group now stopped by her locker to compliment her eyeshadow. She didn't have the heart to admit that the hours of sleep she lost every morning had been pointless so far, or that her anxiety had graduated from the soft buzz of one bee to the frenzy of a whole hive.

She was always a loner, socially awkward and able to slip in and out of any room unseen. The one time she was noticed during her freshman year, it was by Bailey, a sophomore cheerleader who lived one bus stop away. On Aliyah's first day of school, she wandered through the bus trying to find a place. She stopped near Bailey and her noisy entourage, drawn by their high-pitched laughter. Bailey locked her eyes on Aliyah like fresh prey before the surrounding group followed suit. The back of the bus was silent as it lurched forward again.

"Can I help you?" Bailey's voice was sweet as sugar while a few girls around her giggled behind their fresh manicures.

"Uh...I'm new here. Just trying to find a place to sit." Aliyah couldn't bring herself to ask if the empty seat next to one of the girls was available. She hoped they would sense her helplessness and save her the embarrassment. But Bailey saw the opportunity to make her squirm and took it.

"And what does that have to do with us?" The girls behind Bailey laughed louder now. Aliyah wanted to throw up.

"Well there's an empty seat here and I—"

"No plain Janes in this area," Bailey said. Her friends remained silent this time, perhaps to allow the full weight of her statement to settle on Aliyah. When it did, Aliyah's shoulders visibly deflated. "There's a few empty seats in the back." And just like that Aliyah was dismissed, "plain Jane" branded like a scarlet letter. This was when the buzzing between her ears began.

Aliyah thought of Bailey and her group for that entire school day, their perfectly arched eyebrows and airbrushed faces, their hair in long silk presses and expensive sew-ins. She promised herself on the bus ride home that she would become one of them, learn their secrets and slip into the group with the same level of stealth in which she could leave a room unnoticed. Two years later, Aliyah *had* become one of them, but only in looks. Her assimilation to their Barbie standards hadn't led to their acceptance. She boarded the bus each school day, beautiful and by herself.

Halfway through her junior year and after Christmas break, Aliyah climbed the bus stairs, acknowledged the driver with her usual silent nod. She shuffled back to her seat only to find a new girl already there, a transfer student. Her hair was in a beautiful afro, and Aliyah could see her cheeks lightly dusted with a purplish blush. She looked up from her phone to meet Aliyah's confused gaze, her eyes the same dark brown shade.

"Oh, I'm so sorry! Is this your seat? I can move!" The new girl made to sling her bookbag onto her back and stand, but Aliyah stopped her.

"No, it's okay. I can find another seat."

"Or we can sit together! I don't mind." The new girl shifted her bag to the floor, letting Aliyah decide. Aliyah felt a smile forming but tried to hide her excitement.

"What's your name?" Aliyah asked as she slid into the seat beside her.

"Jasmine," she responded. But before she said anything more about herself, she leaned in to examine Aliyah's face. "Is that the new Fenty foundation? I've been thinking about buying it!"

Aliyah let herself smile fully. The buzzing in her head turned down slightly, and she felt it.

Taylor Byas, Ph.D. (she/her), is a Black Chicago native living in Cincinnati, Ohio. She has authored two chapbooks and her debut full-length *I Done Clicked My Heels Three Times*, which has won multiple awards. She is also a co-editor of *Poemhood: Our Black Revivial*, a YA poetry anthology.

Am I Okay? // Tamara Belko

I was fearless. Until I wasn't. I had been tumbling, flipping backwards, a springy slinky for years, until my spring sprung, and, suddenly, I was a misused toy tumbling down the steps, overpowered, out of control and thump! I crashed into the mat, crumpling like a rag doll.

Ten years of gymnastics, ten years of falling and getting back up, and today I lay on my back, breath knocked from my lungs, staring up at the bright gym lights and decided to just stay down.

"Are you okay?" Faces loomed over me, my coach, my teammates. I contemplated the question. *Was I okay? Was I okay?* Slowly, I pushed myself up. Nothing seemed broken. *So, I guess, yes?*

Still, Coach had me sit out the rest of practice. She called my mom, told her I was fine, not concussed, but I'd probably be sore for a few days. Sore. Is that what you call it when you've hurtled through the air and landed on your head? Yup, I was sore alright. I'd whipped-lashed myself with my own body. It would be funny, if it didn't hurt so badly.

I recovered. Sort of …

After a few days, I could turn my neck without shooting pain racing from my shoulders to the top of my head. I even returned to practice. Not to tumbling, but to burpees and planks. To running laps and squats. Ten years of tumbling, ten years of falling and getting back up. But this time … this time, I just couldn't. I couldn't get back to what I had loved for so long.

****

Later, my mom, hands on my shoulders, would say, "I'm proud of you. It's okay to be afraid." I would blink back tears, press my palms to my eyes.

"I don't think I can do it, Mom."

"It's okay," she said and pulled me into her arms. I let the tears fall. *I was not okay.*

Later still, Coach said, "It's like riding a bike. You fall but you have to get back on."

"I don't think I can. I'm not ready."

So Coach allowed me to remove the back tumbling pass from my routine at the next meet.

And the next meet.

And the next meet.
And the next meet.

Now.
I tell myself, *This time. This time. This meet. I will be ready.*
But tumbling isn't like getting back on a horse, a bike, however the hell the saying goes. It isn't. Not for me.
Instead, there is heat rushing through my body and pulsing in my ears. My chest is constricting, and I am choking. I'm choking! I'm going to vomit! No, I am going to die. I'm, literally, going to die if I add the back tumbling pass.
This is death.
This is fear. I don't want this fear.
And so, I don't do it. I don't add the tumbling pass to my routine. I don't back tumble. No back handsprings, no back layouts.
I just … I just need to walk away.
So, I walk away. I walk away from what I once loved because this fear is crippling me, shredding me.
And, yes, I am okay with it. I'm finally really okay.

Tamara Belko is a reader, writer and teacher. As a middle school English teacher and Power of the Pen Creative writing coach, Tamara has spent her career sharing her passion for reading, writing and poetry with her students. Tamara is the author of young adult novel *Perchance to Dream*.

Just Love

poetry· flash fiction · essays

Just
poetry

love   land   world   futures   being

Daniel, My Brother // Federico Erebia
An excerpt from *Pedro & Daniel* (Levine Querido 2023)

Daniel is leaving tomorrow on a plane.

It reminds me of the melancholic lyrics to "Daniel" by Bernie Taupin, hauntingly sung by Elton John.

Released when he was ten years old, I have always thought the song was written . . . for me, about Daniel . . . my -brother.

Though he is younger, not older than me, it speaks of pain, scars that won't heal, and Daniel's eyes.

Daniel's eyes.

When I first heard it, I thought Daniel died in the song, and I cried and cried.

Daniel, my own -brother, had almost died a few years before, and the emotional trauma was still a fresh wound — a scar that hadn't healed.

It seemed as if the songwriting duo knew about me and Daniel, about our shared histories, about our brotherly bond that -won't be broken.

My eyes have cried.

Tears in my eyes have always come easy and quickly for me.

It's been a -great annoyance and embarrassment all my life.

I've seen it as a sign of weakness, but I'm starting to believe they mean I care so much about Daniel, I just -can't hold my tears in.

I know his journey -will differ from that in the song.

Tears -will cloud my eyes when I see Daniel waving goodbye tomorrow.

I will miss him very much.

Federico Erebia, a retired physician, woodworker, author, poet, and illustrator, is the recipient of the 2024 Lambda Literary Award for Exceptional New Writer. His debut novel, *Pedro & Daniel* (Levine Querido 2023), has received awards and other critical acclaim. He lives in Massachusetts with his husband. He suggests comparing Bernie Taupin's lyrics, Elton John's song, and the passage above.

Runaway // Emanuel Xavier

There is a world out there where I belong:
loved by a mother and father who understand
my dreams, who listen to my fears of my older

cousin, his touch, or how boys make fun of me
in school. There is a world out there where I can
grow up to love myself and others like me, where

soft-spoken boys can speak boldly. I will
call it poetry, each memory an inspiration. All
this pain, these dismembered and abandoned cars,

these empty lots left behind where I know deep
in my heart that there is innocence in playing
with dolls, reaching for rainbows, books, even *Mami's*

pretty dresses. I will not be alone in this world.
I have somewhere to run. I do not know exactly
where. I have no maps or stars to guide me through

the night. If it turns out that this is my world,
maybe I should simply learn to laugh and live
and let the others catch up to me instead.

Emanuel Xavier is author of several poetry books including *Selected Poems of Emanuel Xavier* and *Love(ly) Child*. His books have been finalists for International Latino Book Awards and Lambda Literary Awards and his work has appeared in Poetry, A Gathering of the Tribes, Best American Poetry, and elsewhere.

landrover // Laura Kumicz

in the corner of my young eyes i saw your fingers,
tapping and bumping against your landrover's steering wheel,
"who cares what games we choose" you sing,
your hand chasing those greasy fries in my wendy's paper bag,
"little to win, but nothing to lose".
i would brace for the potholes on my seat, with a dripping burger in my hand,
the taste of acidic ketchup filling up my mouth,
and the waves of CO_2 gas and the michigan cold painting my nose a painful red.

after you've departed i've been at war,
scrimmages with hot smoke and supersonic bullets unfolding as i glance at your ashes,
i remember me, your daughter, holding the box of you, on our last drive.
no music, no processed american grease, no run down trembling engine,
but the shale gray spring sky, the heat in the air teasing us,
appearing, then drawing back to cold,
a kind of cold we would find ourselves in, that we would hate, but we'd endure,
knowing the comfort of each other's existence would pull us through.
my mother's ford focus engine only hums,
and her silence speaks ancient words only the ones left behind can understand.
truth be told i hated how your engine squeaked and faltered
as we zoomed across the roads of your old town.
but it's what you could offer, and i let it be, and you let me be, be whatever i wanted to be.
and how will i ever see these same old roads in the way i saw them with you?
that's the problem, i can't.
we simply were, what we were, and nothing could ever change that

Laura Kuzmicz is a young writer who has just graduated with a BA in English Writing and Journalism from Aquinas College in Grand Rapids Michigan, her hometown. In her spare time, she writes fiction and poetry, mainly focusing on grief, magical realism, and unique femininity. Laura is also an aspiring screenwriter.

Between Boys // Valerie Hunter

Once upon a time,
Emmy and Layla were inseparable,
but now Emmy only talks to Layla
when she's between boys,
heartbroken and in need of a therapist.
Layla listens sympathetically
to whatever this villain-boy
has done, then reassures Emmy
that she's still gorgeous, funny, on-trend, loveable,
that whatever faults the boy has found
in her are all his own invention,
that Emmy is so much better than
Kyle-Tariq-Sal-Chris-Diego-whoever-it-is,
that no, she shouldn't apologize to him,
change herself for him, send him pictures
of her boobs, or waste any more tears
over this failed relationship.

It's hard work getting all those stupid boy toxins
out of Emmy's system, requires a lot of repetition
and kindness and sometimes a bit of shouting,
but in the end she always manages to talk Emmy down,
talk her back to being the old Emmy.
They have a week or so of beautiful friendship—
goofing off at the park,
belting out Beyoncé in Emmy's basement,
baking butterscotch brownies,
laughing at dumb videos—
until Emmy abandons her for yet another disaster of a boy,
and Layla is once again alone in the cafeteria,
wishing she had someone
who could detox her from Emmy.

Valerie Hunter teaches high school English and has an MFA in writing for children and young adults from Vermont College of Fine Arts. Her stories and poems have appeared in magazines such as *Cricket*, *Cicada*, and *Paper Lanterns*, and anthologies including *I Sing: The Body* and *Brave New Girls*.

Árbol // Emanuel Xavier

There came a day when it was
decided it was time for you to be cut
down. And so they pulled you apart,
destroyed your bark for sharing
truths. They took one of your roots
and left you scarred for life. A life
that would continue. When they
noticed you stood your ground and
again survived, the forest mocked
and discredited you. Your soul cried
out. But your resilience was never
taken into account. Instead, the rain
washed away your fears, cleansed
your wounds with her delicate touch.
Pink flowers blossomed from your
stems in spite of lack of light and
infertile soil. And as you grew taller
and left them behind, the sun glowed
bigger and brighter bursting from
the sky and birds settled onto your
branches. You nurtured their
passion, provided comfortable
retreat. Your journey out into
the world would be their stories.

Emanuel Xavier is author of several poetry books including *Selected Poems of Emanuel Xavier* and *Love(ly) Child*. His books have been finalists for International Latino Book Awards and Lambda Literary Awards and his work has appeared in Poetry, A Gathering of the Tribes, Best American Poetry, and elsewhere.

Couples Skate // Karen J. Weyant

When the lights dimmed, we knew
to start looking for a partner, and I
always picked the same one: a boy
with dark hair and a shy smile.
We reached for each other, our hands
not yet sweaty, our strides on the rink
confident and sure as we moved
to Air Supply and REO Speedwagon,
groups we made fun of, but whose songs
were perfect for slow skating.
The Disco ball threw silver onto
the hardwood floor, the black light
made everything white, glow.
Once, I saw a girl flaunt her bra
when it shone bright underneath
her thin crocheted sweater.
But I wasn't so bold. For days before
every roller skate rink excursion,
I tried on different outfits, making sure
the same thing didn't happen to me.
Still, whenever I skated with that
boy, the one with dark hair
and a shy smile, I hunched over
trying to hide myself, even though
he stared straight ahead, seldom
really looking my way.

Karen J. Weyant's first full-length collection, *Avoiding the Rapture* was published last fall by Riot in Your Throat press. Her poems have appeared in *Crab Orchard Review, Copper Nickel, Harpur Palate, Fourth River, Lake Effect, Rattle, River Styx* and *Slipstream*. She lives, reads and writes in Northern Pennsylvania but is an Associate Professor of English at Jamestown Community College in Jamestown, New York.

Fill Me // Joe Bisicchia

I don't want to be empty.
Don't want to be lost.
I want to be Yours.

And so,
for the long march,
Lord, make me Your shoe.

Make me that way worn,
that way creased,
that way used.

My skin may wrinkle.
Leather may turn
like leaves.
But with You, I am
an indestructible spring.

And, all along,
not a torn sole at all
but one forever new.

Fill me.
Bring me to being.

And let us march
through the dust,
the mud,
the broken glass,
the glitter,
the morning dew.

Joe Bisicchia has nearly four decades of experience in language arts, from journalism and broadcasting, to teaching, marketing, public affairs, and poetry. An Honorable Mention recipient for the Fernando Rielo XXXII World Prize for Mystical Poetry, he has written four published collections of poetry.

Graduation // Chris Crowe

"Death lies on her like an untimely frost
Upon the sweetest flower of all the field."

Ella, your friends and classmates,
somber and silly, crowd the auditorium
ready to be launched into the world.
Capped, gowned, and
seated in alphabetical order,
they wait to be called
to stroll across the platform for a
handshake and diploma, to
bask, briefly, in the collective
attention of family and friends.

Speeches are made,
names are read,
students move up and down,
and we wait and wait and wait
for our turn to cheer your
transition from child to adult.

But, Ella, your seat isn't saved,
your name isn't read,
your diploma isn't awarded, and
while your classmates celebrate
graduation, we can only
remember and savor
the fourteen radiant years
of sunshine you shared with us.

Christopher Crowe is an American professor of English and English education at Brigham Young University specializing in young adult literature. In addition to his academic work, Crowe also writes books for the young-adult market, including *Mississippi Trial, 1955*.

Haibun: My Girlfriend's House // Laura Shovan

The first time I have dinner with her family, it's chaos. She has too many brothers and I have none. Her father is a megaphone — blasting jokes, opinions, questions over beef stew. *What do your parents do? What are young going to study in college? Play any sports?* There are six of us at the table, everyone's hands reaching and grabbing. *You had two rolls already, that's mine!* Only her mother is calm, spooning stew into her mouth. She speaks underneath the noise: *Why don't you two go for a walk? The boys will clear up.* The uproar! They're still complaining as we slip out the door. There's an abandoned house my girlfriend wants to show me. She takes my hand, leads me to twin tire tracks through the woods. The sun is setting on the mossy house. She points to the yellow paint and white curtains printed with flowers. *Someone lived here,* she says. *Someone cared about this place.* But to me, the house is like a pat of butter, melting, and the woods are hungry for something to tear apart.

Beware of Dog sign
fused to tree trunk's thick bark
silent forest

Laura Shovan is a Pushcart Prize nominated poet and a middle grade novelist. Among her award-winning children's books are *The Last Fifth Grade of Emerson Elementary*, *Takedown*, and *A Place at the Table*, written with Saadia Faruqi. Laura is a longtime poet-in-the-schools. She teaches at Vermont College of Fine Arts.

Alienated // Emanuel Xavier

Lights from a galaxy
could take billions of years to reach
me/us/them
racism from a stranger's milky way
only takes seconds

I/we remember the first time
I/we experienced hatred
estranged thanks to this other skin
How lonely it is out in space
fathered in mystery; lost in unholy lure

We/they were here
It is phenomenon that I/we even survive
Histories still unfolding
Will I/we/they be rewritten like slavery?
The Holocaust? Witches?

Freedom and idealized beauty must feel divine
as far & as distant as stars
for me/us/them

Emanuel Xavier is author of several poetry books including *Selected Poems of Emanuel Xavier* and *Love(ly) Child*. His books have been finalists for International Latino Book Awards and Lambda Literary Awards and his work has appeared in Poetry, A Gathering of the Tribes, Best American Poetry, and elsewhere.

Just essays

love   land   world   futures   being

Remember // Jennifer Guyor Jowett

Remember when you were in kindergarten and riding home in the back of the nearly empty bus. You overheard two third grade boys in the seat across from you. They kept glancing at you and talking about kissing *you*, and you shifted uncomfortably, angling your neck so that your eyes could peek over the high seat back, looking for the driver, who kept her own eyes on the dirt of Bartlett Rd, naturally. And then one grinned, wickedly, in your direction, before leaning over, pressing warm, wet lips against your cheek, which flamed a red, hot heat and you could say nothing. You were too little and your voice wasn't yet formed.

Remember just a couple years later when school let out and the line of big yellow buses stretched like train cars all along Orchard Street between your Catholic school and the junior high and elementary schools parked kiddy-corner and opposite. Kids of all ages tumbled from doorways and down steps in a rush to leave, chattering and yelling, shoving and running. You wove your way along the sidewalk where those rushing from every which school fought to find a place to climb aboard the same buses. You were nearly there, foot poised in the empty air of the step to board when you heard the boys call. "Catlicker. Catlicker." And you knew they meant to draw notice that you were not of them and they were not of you. Yet you turned to look anyway, for just a second, one second, mouth parted. Their sneers of disdain at your uniform silenced any thought of protest before it could really form.

Remember the school dance when RL, separating himself from the boys on one side of the room, asked JM to dance. She had a crush on him and we'd all been hoping he'd ask her. When she said yes, he glanced back at the herd with just a hint of a smile. And they shared looks and toothy grins before quarters exchanged hands. The outrage you felt only increased a song ending later when he returned to his side of the room and held out his own hand as all the girls watched. JM turned away. Mortified. A few dances later, he approached you, asking, and you turned him down with a question of your own - *Do you really need another quarter?* You had no intention of being part of their scheming, still felt offended on behalf of your friend. And the words rose up, after years of being silenced, knowing that mortifications and indignities would no longer, could no longer, abrade your soul or anyone else's, and your voice found its way.

Jennifer Guyor Jowett teases stories and writers into being. She is the author of *Into the Shadows*, a middle grade historical fiction based on true-life events, the creator of the #dogearedbookaward, and a defender of fierce girls. Jennifer is a 7th/8th ELA teacher in the mitten state.

Ready // Kate Sjostrom

His left hand steadying the steering wheel, Jon reaches with his right to eject, flip, then re-insert the mix-tape he's made for me. In the seconds before the music begins, I consult the cassette case to see what's next: a song by Muddy Waters.

Piano is quickly joined by drums, then bass, then harmonica, then Jon, who turns to me, smiling, as he sings along to "I'm Ready."

I smile back, then we both look ahead into the remarkably uncongested lane before us on the main expressway out of the city. It is just shy of 8:00 a.m. on a Sunday. On a holiday.

It's funny, I think. Last year — and the year before and the year before that one — I would have been heading home at this time, too, but from the Easter Sunrise Service at our church, not from the Maxwell Street Market. Neither my mom nor my siblings wanted to get up for the 5:00 a.m. service this year, and my dad's not around to make us, but I still haven't digested the fact that my mom let me leave the house on a holiday, let alone with a boy two years older than me, even if it is a pre-breakfast outing to browse the stalls at a street market.

Breakfast. That is one reason I'm sorry to miss the Sunrise Service. After the mass, an older parishioner, George, always puts on the greatest breakfast. Mounds of fresh fruit ringed with palm fronds, island volcanos erupting pineapple, melons, strawberries. What always gets me is the coconut. Not the shredded kind for baking (the kind I steal by the handful when there are no other sweets in the house). Chunks of real coconut, some still in their hairy brown husks. My stomach longs for them — for anything, really. I should have said yes when Jon offered to buy tamales at the market, but I hate for a boy to watch me eat.

I wonder what we'll have for breakfast at home this morning. I wonder, too, if the morning will have gotten started without me, then remember that my siblings are on college time, so there's no way. Also, I remember that nothing gets started before the Easter basket hunt, and I know they won't start *that* without me. I'm fourteen and out with a boy, but I'm still the baby, and I have no doubt the basket hunt this year is largely for my sake; otherwise, my sister Monica wouldn't have snuck away to fill the baskets out of my sight last night, and my mom wouldn't have whispered over the phone last week, "I'll buy the candy, but I'm not filling the baskets; I always hated that." Past tense. Something is over.

Jon again takes his right hand from the steering wheel, this time to take one of my hair's waves into it and sing with Muddy Waters about good-looking girls with hair like mine. Then he returns his hand to the wheel and starts explaining that a lot of people think this is a Buddy Guy song, don't realize that his is a cover. I nod, as I have done frequently this morning. This tape, this outing, is clearly meant to be an education. Jon couldn't believe I'd never been to Maxwell Street, instructed me that early morning is the best time to go so vendors don't think you're just another *Blues Brothers* tourist. So much for me to learn.

And yet he'd gone on about how he likes me because I'm so well-read and know so much about art and music (if not the blues). That's why, he had told me as we surveyed the incense burners at one of the market stalls, he so wishes he wasn't fresh out of a long-term relationship. If he were ready for a relationship, I'd be just what he wanted. Yes, this morning *has* been an education.

Jon turns up the volume and growl-sings with Muddy Waters about how ready he is. I look to my lap where I've cradled the incense burner I'd finally chosen: a black painted skull with a hole in the top of its head for the wooden bottom of an incense stick. I lift it, surprised again by its heft, consolation in the face of what seems, upon closer inspection, to be a bad paint job.

Jon stops singing to ask, "What are you going to name him?" Reading my confusion, he looks to the incense holder in my hands. "You've got to give him a name."

Like so many things Jon has said today, this suggestion is somehow charming. And like always, I want what I say to impress, to set me apart from the likes of ex-girlfriends one isn't quite over. Jon's already decided the black skull is a boy's and so I scan the boys' names in my mind, trying to push past the names of cousins and classmates, all too conventional. I browse book characters for novel names. And then it just comes to me.

"Atticus," I say.

"Perfect." Jon signals to exit the expressway, nodding in approval.

I don't admit I haven't read *To Kill a Mockingbird* or even seen the movie, nor that I know nothing about Atticus except that he is the admired dad in the story. Mostly, I've just heard the name and thought it sufficiently unique to impress Jon, which it has. And I like the sound of it. *Atticus,* I say in my head, looking at the imperfectly painted black skull in my hand. Having named him, I feel protective of him, hold him a little more gently, draw my thumb softly across his plaster forehead as if to wipe clean his memory of a life before me.

Kate Sjostrom is a writer and writing teacher educator based in Oak Park, IL. Her work has been published in *Rhyme & Rhythm: Poems for Student Athletes*, *RHINO*, *English Journal*, and elsewhere.

Twan't Much // Lee Martin

At the tire repairs factory, I knew a man named Jack who had no teeth, who brought the same thing for lunch every day, a fried egg sandwich in a wrinkled and stained paper bag. He had a family he could barely support, one that didn't have, as my father often said, "as much as a pot to piss in." This was in 1976, a time of double-digit inflation and high interest rates in a small Midwestern town going nowhere fast.

One day, Friday the week of Christmas, I brought Jack a platter of homemade cookies. I gave it to him in the parking lot after work. "For you and your family," I said, certain he'd be pleased.

I was twenty-one and saving money to go back to college. I had no idea that my gift would call attention to the fact that Jack's life would more than likely always be exactly what it was at that moment. He was a poor man with poor prospects.

He bowed his head. He held that platter in his big hands, calloused and scarred, the knuckles all knobbed up, and he mumbled, "Much obliged." Then he walked away, leaving me to feel the embarrassment I'd caused him, the shame.

The next day, my wife and I found a box of Whitman's chocolates leaning against our front door. No card. No note of explanation. But I knew right away that Jack had left them for us.

The factory held its Christmas party at the Elks Lodge that evening, and I watched him get drunk on free liquor, so drunk that toward the end of the evening he was sick outside the bathroom, and his wife had to ask for help hauling him to the car.

Come Monday, he was back at work, cutting slabs of rubber from the mill drum. I never said a word to him about those Whitman chocolates, nor did I tell him that I wished that I or someone else had told him to lay off the booze that night at the party, to let him know he didn't need to ruin what was a fine evening for his wife — a prime rib dinner, a few spins around the dance floor — and that was sure as heck what he was going to do if he kept guzzling that bourbon. How in the hell would you say that to a man ground down by work and the circumstances of his life on a night when he had a chance to cut loose, when the liquor was free, and for at least a little while, so was he?

Well, you don't say it. That's what. I regretted the gift of the cookies and all it had wrought, so I kept my yap shut.

Then the day comes when I'm back in college, and I'm in a theatre class, and one day I'm performing in a scene from *Our Town*. It's the scene at the end of the play when the Webbs' daughter, Emily, is granted her wish to come back from the dead and relive one day of her life. She chooses her twelfth birthday. February 11, 1899.

I play Constable Warren, who meets up with Emily's father, the newspaper editor, outside on the street as he's coming home from the train station. My character has been out early to rescue a drunk, asleep in a snowdrift near Polish Town. Constable Warren has been doing his work on a morning when it's ten degrees below zero. He's saved a man's life, but still he doesn't mean much of anything to the give and take of the Webb family that morning. He's just a minor character, a simple man of duty, on the periphery of their lives.

I have a line at the end of the scene, a line I've worked over and over, trying to get it to please me. Constable Warren, when Mr. Webb says he'll have to put word of that rescue up near Polish Town in the newspaper, says, "Twan't much." I want just the right balance of humility and pride and unease. Just the right hint of things unsaid, things I learned from a work-worn man one Christmas season when neither of us knew that he had anything to teach me.

"Twan't much," I say.

The next thing is easy. The exit. All I have to do is leave.

Lee Martin is the author of fifteen books, including the Pulitzer Prize Finalist novel, *The Bright Forever*. He teaches in the MFA in Creative Writing Program at The Ohio State University and the Naslund-Mann School of Writing at Spalding University.

"Twan't Much" originally appeared in *Brevity* and in *Such a Life* (University of Nebraska Press).

Founding Haiku Festival // Regina Harris Baiocchi

In December 2000, when the Illinois Poet Laureate Gwendolyn Brooks passed away, I was hurled back to the day we met. I was seven years old. Ms. Brooks was hosting a poetry reading for kids. She gave some of us cash awards for our poems. I mailed a thank-you note to her home at 7428 South Evans, Chicago, 60619. She replied.

Fond memories of reading my poem to Ms. Brooks stayed with me. I sent her more poems.

She replied each time. We became pen pals, then she mentored me through my high school, undergrad, and grad school years.

In my first teaching job I read aloud to my junior high homeroom class. Students loved Gwendolyn Brooks's "We Real Cool," Emily Dickinson's "314" (Hope is the thing with feathers) Langston Hughes's "Dream Variations" and "I, Too". I read Jewelle Gomez's "Swimming Lesson," Toni Cade Bambara's "Lesson" from *Gorilla, My Love,* and J. D. Sallinger's *Catcher in the Rye.* Students discussed Henry David Thoreau's *Walking,* and other classics I read to them.

Reading aloud helped sharpen students' listening skills. Students escaped the day's rigors and enjoyed literature without the burden of being tested for a grade.

When I invited Ms. Brooks to do a poetry reading for my 100 students, the audience grew to 800 K-8 students and teachers. We planned a thirty-minute reading followed by Q&A. Ms. Brooks recited "We Real Cool," "Song in the Front Yard," "Life of Lincoln West," et al. When a student requested an autograph, Ms. Brooks asked, "Would anyone else like an autograph?"

Every hand in the assembly was raised. During the first hour of signing autographs, parents who had come to collect their kids scurried to bookstores and bought books to be signed. Passersby joined the line stretching outside our school. I asked Ms. Brooks if she wanted to rest. She sipped water and vowed, "As long as kids want my chicken scratch, I'll keep writing."

Ms. Brooks had a distinctive penmanship that reflected her big heart. Her 1:30 to 2:30 visit ended well after 7:00 PM. She signed the last autograph as cheerfully as she had signed the first. I offered to increase her fee to reflect her extended stay. She graciously declined. I will always remember her generosity. For years Ms.

Brooks fondly recalled the afternoon she spent signing notebook paper, books, and one girl's diary.

Inspired by Ms. Brooks, I founded Haiku Festival in 2004. Haiku Festival's mission is to "celebrate youth through poetry and promote literacy." This mission is important to me and my co-founder, Greg Baiocchi. We are avid readers, as were our parents and grandparents. Haiku Festival is our heart child. I am responsible for the arts. Greg is our IT brainiac.

This year marks Haiku Festival Chicago's 20th anniversary. Each year a panel of judges blindly names winners from submissions we receive. In April, National Poetry Month, 8-to-14-year-olds present their winning haiku, nōtan, and essays; and 13-to-18-year-olds present essays at Haiku Festival's awards program. Winners receive cash awards, books, and bragging rights. Our programs also feature young musicians, taiko drummers, and a guest poet.

Our first year we received original haiku from 75 Chicago poets. By 2005, 150 youth replied to our Call for Poetry. Each year the number of submissions grows exponentially, and hails from more states and countries. In 2014, we published *Haiku Festival's 10th Anniversary Anthology* and hosted haiku master, Prof. Sonia Sanchez from Temple University.

This year nearly 1,400 poets submitted haiku. We published *Haiku Festival 20th Anniversary Anthology*, dedicated "to Gwendolyn Elizabeth Brooks Blakely, Illinois Poet Laureate, and Pulitzer Prize Winner." Our anthology features 107 award-winning haiku, 3 essays, 1 prose poem, and 12 nōtan designs. In two decades, Haiku Festival has received over 37,000 haiku from around the world.

When I began writing poetry at age seven, my teachers introduced haiku and other forms. I gravitated toward haiku. I love haiku's brevity, subtlety, and that it is a contraction of the phrase *haikai no ku* ("light verse"). "Hai" is Japanese for "amusement" and "ku" means "verse" or poem. (Haiku is often called *ku*.)

Haiku are generally 3-line unrhymed nature poems of up to 17 syllables (5/7/5 form). Haiku use irony, or an aha moment. Early haiku introduced longer poems called renga. My love for reading and writing haiku led to six related forms.

Like haiku, **senryū** are 3-line unrhymed poems up to 17 syllables (5/7/5). Haiku are about nature; senryū are about human nature.

Renga is linked poetry written by 2 or more poets. The first poet writes haiku; the second replies with two lines of seven syllables each: 5/7/5 followed by 7/7, another 5/7/5, then 7/7, etc. Some renga chains go on for years, across different countries.

Tanka is a 5-line poem of up to 31 syllables: 5/7/5 (upper poem: concrete ideas) plus 7/7 (lower poem: emotional aspects). Tanka is written by one person.

Other haiku-related forms include **haibun**, hybrid of prose (paragraph) and haiku; **cherita**, a 6-line poem in 3 stanzas; and monoku, 1-line horizontal, vertical, or diagonal ku up to 17 syllables. (NB: "haiku" is plural *and* singular, like its related forms. No "s" is used.)

Haiku Festival Chicago offers workshops to teach participants how to read, write, and publish haiku, senryū, renga, tanka, haibun, cherita, and monoku. For samples of all 7 forms, to book a reading, workshop, or to answer our Call for Poetry, visit www.HaikuFest.com or email regina@haikufest.com

Regina Harris Baiocchi is a composer, author, and poet. Her music is recorded and performed by renowned orchestras and acclaimed artists. Her byline appears in *Modern Haiku, Obsidian, Fire This Time,* and elsewhere. She wrote *urban haiku, blues haiku,* and *at the gate of the sun.* Regina's fiction includes *Indigo Sound, Finding Déjà,* and *Scuppernong.*

Just fiction

love land world futures being

Bittersweet // Kennedy Essmiller

Laura's arms wrapped around her torso as if they were the only things preventing her insides from spilling out onto the pristine white tiles that covered her mother's kitchen. Ingredients for cupcakes covered the stone counter island above her, seemingly forgotten as she leaned her head forward onto her knees. The nausea would pass, you knew, but the time it took before it passed was hell on her. She had finally gotten her breathing back under control; hugging herself usually helped her steady her breaths.

If you were in a different place, at a different time, your hugs also would help. But you knew that touching her in her family's house would only serve to ramp up her anxiety, not calm it.

Letting out a deep breath, Laura sat back up and let her arms fall to her sides. She looked down at her toes. The second one was longer than the first one, which made her feel self-conscious being barefoot around other people, even you. She tucked her toes underneath herself, removing them from her vision as well as yours.

"How are you feeling?" you asked, venturing from your position leaning against the counter to join her, legs crisscrossed against the cold floor.

"Fine," she said, standing up as you slid to the ground. You were left staring at her calves rather than her face.

She gulped down what was left of her now-warm Diet Coke before tossing the can into the trash at the foot of the island. Clapping her hands together in front of her, she turned to the task at hand.

"Alright," she muttered. "Cupcakes."

Laura had begged for your help in baking two dozen cupcakes for a fundraiser for the local library. She didn't need the help, and even if she did, you would probably be one of the last people she turned to. But you had a sneaking suspicion that she was looking for an excuse to be in the same room with you — even if it meant you burning or otherwise ruining the desserts she had promised the struggling library.

Laura's apartment only had a stove and no oven, and your oven could fit half a dozen cookies or cupcakes at a time at most. So, you went to her parents' house across town to borrow their kitchen.

Her parents were home, despite Laura's belief otherwise. When she referred to you as her "friend" rather than her "girlfriend" in front of them, despite telling you months back she had told them the truth, you had fallen silent. When they left the kitchen, the two of you had a hushed argument.

"You said you told them!" you whispered, the moment her parents were out of earshot. "You said they loved that I was your girlfriend, and that they couldn't wait to have us over for dinner!"

"I know," she said. "I meant to, really, I did! I just — I couldn't."

"What were you planning on doing when we showed up tonight? Why did you even invite me?"

Evidently, she hadn't expected her parents to be home or to return at any point in the evening. "They told me they were going to a dinner party to celebrate their friend's promotion."

At that point, you said something along the lines of being tired of feeling like a dirty secret and wanting to be with someone who was proud to call you their girlfriend and partner.

You hadn't exactly told her that you wanted to break up. Clearly, though, she filled in the blanks, because she immediately slipped down to the ground, her breathing panicked.

Now, you didn't speak as you began making the cupcakes.

While she focused on whisking the dry ingredients together, you focused on mixing the wet ingredients together in a separate bowl. Cracking the eggs was always your favorite part — you loved the feel of the fragile eggshell crumbling in your hands after the egg slicked out into the bowl.

Once the batter was mixed thoroughly, Laura poured about half the bag of bittersweet chocolate chunks into the mixture. Some of the larger pieces began to sink like rocks in molasses, but some of them still needed some encouragement. Using a wooden spoon, she slowly mixed the pieces in until the chunks seemed to be distributed evenly, looking like freckles dotting pale skin.

While one batch cooked, you made the batter for the next batch. The timer dinged, and you switched the pans out, the entire time refusing to be the first to speak.

Wordlessly, Laura handed you the shaker of assorted sprinkles, and you began shaking tiny pink and blue butterflies onto the frosted cupcakes after careful consideration.

"You have to understand," Laura said quietly without looking over at you. "I have no idea how they'll react. I'm just trying to find the right moment."

You focused your attention on a stray butterfly that had fallen into a blob of forgotten frosting on the counter. Half of its pink body was submerged in a chocolate sludge. Only one wing and antenna were visible. You fought the urge to point out she had had over a year of opportunities, over a year of moments throughout your relationship.

You wanted to point out your past experience with this, help her to understand how this had happened before. You had been burned by this particular fire, and you weren't interested in receiving another scar from it.

Reaching out, Laura slid her fingers over your hand. You wiggled your fingers in response, allowing her to weave her fingers through. You stood like that for several moments, fingers interlocked, slathering cupcakes in frosting and showering them in crystal sprinkles and butterflies. In those moments, you dared to hope. You dared to hope that maybe you would survive this, that maybe you would make it beyond Laura's fear and shame.

Her parents burst back into the kitchen, exclaiming, "Something sure smells good!"

Laura retracted her hand so quickly that her nails scratched your skin.

You tried to ignore the tears that pricked your eyes as Laura laughed and offered a cupcake to each of her parents. Without looking over at her, you stuck your finger out and pushed the butterfly completely into the blob of frosting, submerging it and hiding it from view.

Kennedy Essmiller is a queer writer who earned her MFA in Creative Writing at Oklahoma State University. Her short story, "Mountains" won second place in the University of Western Alabama's 2017 Sucarnochee Review Fiction contest.Her work is published in *Frontier Mosaic* and *The Good Life Review*. You can follow her on Instagram at @kennedywogan.

As Petals Fall on Asphalt Roads // Aimee Parkison

Sometimes there's food on the plate, but no one wants to eat it. No one wants to eat it, but when everyone is hungry, it's gone. It's gone, and there's music playing, piano music in the parlor where everyone's stomach is rumbling, as if talking wordlessly, complaining about the food that is gone. Complaining about the food that is gone, we stare out the windows at the rain battering the rose of Sharon as petals fall on asphalt roads. As petals fall on asphalt roads, the rain pours harder, the piano music stops, and I remember when I was a young child, wondering why my mother never ate at the table, why she only ate alone when everyone else was finished and only if there was food left on the plates, though there often wasn't. Though there often wasn't, I didn't realize why she wasn't eating since because of her artful misdirection I never understood food was in scarce supply in my childhood. Food was in scarce supply in my childhood, but dreams were not on mornings when I woke, remembering the vivid pastel bakery and all the wonderful cakes I had eaten, bright cakes displayed under glass like valuable jeweled sculptures, unlike any cake I had ever seen. Unlike any cake I had ever seen, these dream cakes nourished me when I slept, not realizing I was hungry because of how delicious it was. How delicious it was, even though it wasn't real and would make real food seem undesirable in comparison, as the dream baker in the child's mind could prepare the unconscious food to feed unrecognized hunger. Unrecognized hunger waited like a friend with the dream baker and the dream cakes as my mother entered the bakery as if nothing was wrong with the fact that I was nude and eating all the cakes. Nude and eating all the cakes, I was never so happy until she asked why I had saved none for her.

Aimee Parkison has published eight books and won FC2's Catherine Doctorow Innovative Fiction Prize and *North American Review's* Kurt Vonnegut Prize. She is Professor of Fiction Writing at OSU. Her work has appeared in *North American Review, Puerto Del Sol, Five Points,* and *Best Small Fictions.* www.aimeeparkison.com

A Decent Human // Valerie Hunter

When Cal first went to see Aunt Grace at Morningside Manor, he was eleven years old and cried all the way home. When Mom suggested they not go back, Cal agreed, even though he didn't want to. He always agreed with Mom because she expected him to.

Aunt Grace wasn't his actual aunt, but she was still family, the person Cal always turned to when he needed someone who understood, someone who listened, someone who never expected him to agree with her just for the sake of agreeing. He'd spent countless hours at Aunt Grace's home while his mother was working, and he'd learned so much from her. She made sure Cal knew how to cook, how to identify the stars, how to play checkers, and, most importantly, how to be a decent human.

"Do the right thing, even when it's hard," she always said. "Be kind. And never be afraid to apologize. That's what will make you a decent human."

Cal knew he stopped being a decent human when he agreed not to visit Aunt Grace again. For five years he tried not to think about that, or about her, but it was impossible.

When Cal turned sixteen, he realized he was sick of being a less-than-decent human. The next day he took the bus to Morningside Manor after school, asked for Grace Touhy, and released a breath he hadn't realized he'd been holding when the woman at the desk gave him a room number. His relief was short-lived; when he went to the room, he didn't see Aunt Grace, just a tiny husk of a woman with empty eyes. Cal suddenly remembered why he'd cried after that first visit, how this place bled the Aunt Graceness out of Aunt Grace.

Still, he forced himself to sit, take her hand, and talk to her. Instead of asking Aunt Grace if she remembered him—she clearly didn't—he pumped her full of memories, reminiscing about the meals they'd prepared together, the solar system she'd helped him create for a fifth grade science project, the manga series they'd both devoured. But Aunt Grace just shut her eyes, like she was tired of him. Or worse, like she didn't even realize he was there.

Afterwards Cal felt like crying, just like last time. But sixteen-year-old boys couldn't cry on public buses, and by the time he got home it was suppertime, so he couldn't cry then, either, not in front of Mom. When he was finally alone in his room, an acceptable place to leak out the day's emotions, it was too late. The tears were stuck in his head like glue, and he had no release from his sadness.

He went back the following week with a potted violet. Aunt Grace used to have a garden, a riot of color that Cal took for granted until the new people moved in. Now there were just shrubs, always slightly brown.

Aunt Grace looked at the plant the way Cal wished she'd look at him. "Viola papilionacea," she said finally. It sounded like a disease, but when

Cal Googled it he discovered it was the violet's scientific name. He tried to be impressed rather than disappointed that Aunt Grace remembered the flower's name but not his.

The next week the violet was gone. Cal couldn't get up the nerve to ask the woman at the desk about it. Maybe someone knocked it and broke the pot, or stole it, or threw it away so it wouldn't have to be watered. Regardless, it was gone, and Cal was filled with a simmering fury that Aunt Grace couldn't have something green and flowering.

He vowed to give Aunt Grace flowers she could keep. That evening he dug through his closet until he found the bag he'd stashed there five years ago. It contained seven skeins of yarn in a rainbow of colors, two crochet hooks, and a dozen squares with flowers blooming in the middle, some of them (his) quite wonky, others (Aunt Grace's) perfect.

Aunt Grace had taught him to crochet the last winter she was home. He'd protested at first, saying boys didn't crochet, but she insisted that was nonsense so he reconsidered. He'd enjoyed it, once he got the hang of it — it was a way to work out the day's frustrations through his fingers.

They'd been making an afghan. Aunt Grace's idea, but Cal went along with it, even the flowered pattern she'd chosen. He picked up the hooks now, and was surprised how easily it came back to him — the loops, the pulls, the fastening off. His sadness poured out of his fingers more easily than tears. The blocks were still wonky, but he didn't care, just kept going, one or two a night after he had done his homework or just needed a break. The bright colors sang to him, making him feel like he was warm and safe on Aunt Grace's couch again.

When he finished, the afghan was a rainbow monstrosity, but Cal folded it carefully and took another ride on the bus. He spread the afghan over Aunt Grace's bed, over the small lump in the bed that was Aunt Grace, and watched her run her hands over all the colors and then beam, perhaps in pure happiness that colors still existed in the world, that flowers could still bloom, even in this drab room. Cal sat and talked — not memories this time, just the humdrum of his day — and he didn't care that Aunt Grace never looked at him, that she couldn't take her eyes off the crocheted flowers.

Maybe, deep down in that part of her mind that still knew the scientific name of the violet, she recognized the afghan for what it was: both an apology and a thank you. Cal hoped so. She was the most decent human he knew, and he wanted her to know that deep in her bones, where she could never forget.

Valerie Hunter teaches high school English and has an MFA in writing for children and young adults from Vermont College of Fine Arts. Her stories and poems have appeared in magazines such as *Cricket*, *Cicada*, and *Paper Lanterns*, and anthologies including *I Sing: The Body* and *Brave New Girls*.

Natural Selection // S Maxfield

On the day of her fourteenth birthday, she would be expected to choose: Lion or Dove. She had considered this nearly nonstop for the last four years at least. Which familiar would be hers? Each time she felt the choice made, the discarded one would again resurface, clouding her thoughts.

She was told that she was merely confused. She was told that when the time came, her one true choice would become clear. Her naivety would disperse as the surface tension of a pond gives way to a diver, revealing new depths. She was told, "You will just know which one."

One.

The day arrives. She awakes, newly fourteen, with a terrible pit in her stomach. Everyone will soon gather for the ceremony. The elders, her peers, the little ones with plenty of open space still ahead of their choices. Today is the day, and she still cannot discern which call to follow. Is it Lion's thunderous roar, or Dove's lilting song that pulls more deeply? She must choose, but she cannot decide.

A flash of realization: *I want them both.*

The thought shocks her. Abomination.

She wraps her braids high on her head and resolves to choose Lion. It's the more expected choice for someone shaped as she is. She sighs and tries to believe that having finally chosen, Lion's roar will at last drown Dove's song. She assures herself that this longing she feels in two directions will fade. She cannot stay a child forever, and maturity means choosing. It seems everyone says so. Perhaps that is what this ceremony is for. Perhaps everyone feels as she does before their declaration. Her breathing eases. She is comforted by the thought that perhaps she is not so different.

A knock at her door signals that it is time. She pulls on her long ceremonial shift, embroidered with the endless swirls of shining thread she has labored over since her tenth birthday. Her initial dreams of this moment sinking to dread with each passing stitch, as time ran out, and clarity did not come. Now, she walks into the sunlight, where her community has gathered around her. The elders stand, each with their chosen familiar: Dove or Lion. She kneels in the grass, feeling near tears.

She must now bury a part of her heart.

The Selected Elder comes to stand before her and puts up a hand for silence. "This child of our own comes before us today to assert her life's choice, with honesty and without reservation. Child, I address you in the manner of youth for the last time, rise and make your declaration."

She stands. The Selected Elder's words swim in her mind. *Honesty. Without reservation.* Suddenly, a rush of feeling floods her, blocking out everything else. She has become accustomed to shoving her own voice to the soles of her feet, sinking it underground with every step. But, now, her voice rises all the way from her feet, past the pit in her stomach, through her unburied heart, and out of her mouth into the meadow.

"Both. I seek both Lion and Dove."

She hears the community gasp.

But then, perhaps not everyone is scandalized after all? She notices some in the circle seem to view her with particular approval. How had she never noticed those on the fringes who now smile at her? Some even have familiars not approved by the council. Surely that cannot be a Zebra, an Evergreen, a School of Fish? And there, is that not someone without any familiar at all, yet wearing Elders' robes? Could it be that she is different and yet…not alone?

A Dove swoops down and lands on her shoulder just as a Lion nudges a massive mane under her hand. She has chosen both, and both have come to her. There is whispering, but there is also applause. There are raised eyebrows, but there are also arms circling her shoulders. On this day of choosing, she decides to lean into the arms and ignore the eyebrows.

Moments and years go by. Many still tell her that her path is an avoidance, a cheat. They warn that her opposing familiars will destroy each other. She chuckles. She has learned that she needn't stifle her own voice to favor these others. Dove and Lion are harmonious at her side, neither more significant, neither less real. Together, they guide her always, regardless of what others may observe.

A child no longer, she is whole, and she has nothing to prove to anyone.

S Maxfield is a genderqueer, bi+, and disabled writer. Their flash fiction has been published by *WinC Magazine* and *Voyage YA* by Uncharted, and s/he has a short story featured in the anthology *We Mostly Come Out at Night* (Running Press, 2024). linktr.ee/essmaxfield

Promposal // Tamara Belko

In January it is slushy and gray, and moody, vitamin D deficient teens roam the halls half awake and drooling like Zombies. Everyone except one. Nose and cheeks cherry red from the biting wind, he has just arrived and stands like a sentinel at her locker, holding a bouquet of pink roses, punctuated with sprigs of baby's breath. She shrieks, "Yes!" and the sleepy gawkers awake, momentarily, from January crusted apathy, to applaud.

For a moment, I imagine being that bold, holding flowers for my crush. Not roses, but lilies, just like her name. I slink away with ideas of my prom proposal flitting through my head. How will I ask the girl who blows kisses my way as she passess, always bringing heat to my cheeks and a flutter to my stomach?

In February, they hunt for dresses. Frost still clings to windows and billows of breath float in the air. For a beat, the strapless dresses bring summer, and the vibrant swirls of color -- Barbie pink, periwinkle, sapphire blue -- revive the dull days. So many dresses. So many choices. Sweetheart necklines, V-neck, corsets, sequined mesh. Chiffon, satin, tulle, organza. A-line, short, long. While my friends buy their dresses, I continue to imagine how I will ask my crush. The pictures play in my mind: I, personally, deliver the chai tea to her in study hall along with my handmade origami heart invitation. Or, I don't deliver the tea because it probably will be cold by the time it arrives, and I slip the card into her locker when she isn't looking.

Or...I just ask her. Or... I don't.

In March, spring is new, but winter is still hanging on like an old coat, snow blanketing the ground. The cold doesn't stop the girls from buying shoes, strappy and pointy, chunky heels and platforms. Much to the dismay of my friends who advised otherwise, I delivered the chi tea anonymously and stuffed the crushed origami card in my own locker. My crush hurries by and blows me a kiss. I melt instead of finding courage. "Come on, Bella! My friends admonish me. "Just ask her already!"

In April, I wonder *Did I imagine her interest?* She hasn't responded to my casual texts to hang out. Maybe the kisses were meant for someone else to catch. But now she is walking my way. "Hey," she says with a wink and a side bump to my hip. My hip is on fire. My insides are mush.

"Hey," I reply, stuffing my hands deep into my pockets.

"Going to prom?" she asks. Before I can unstick my tongue and form coherent words, she asks, "Do you want to go with me?"

It's May and prom has arrived. Today the question is hair. Curls? Braided. Updo? Ponytail? Side bun? Messy bun? Today the question is also lipstick. I can imagine my friends in the bathroom chittering like excited squirrels as they fumble through their makeup looking for the perfect shades. I don't worry about any of this as I run my hand through my short purple curls, straighten my tie, and slide into black loafers. I wonder if my crush is worried about these things, I hope she isn't because I think she is perfect just the way she is.

It's prom and I have arrived to pick up my crush. Her parents invite me in and my stomach drops to the floor as she emerges in a floral printed fuchsia dress with ruffles cascading to the floor, her long dark hair swooping to the side, revealing a heart shaped birthmark on her right shoulder. My words have left me, and she giggles and winks at my silence.

"You girls look so cute!" Lily's mom says and the camera flashes, catching me in a long blink. "Let's try that again!"

My smile stretches wide. After all the poses and pictures on the double porch swing and by the trellis of climbing blue clematis, we are ready to depart.

I offer Lily my arm and we step outside, head to the car and off to prom.

Tamara Belko is a reader, writer and teacher. As a middle school English teacher and Power of the Pen Creative writing coach, Tamara has spent her career sharing her passion for reading, writing and poetry with her students. Tamara is the author of young adult verse novel *Perchance to Dream.*

Just Land

poetry· flash fiction · essays

Just poetry

love land world futures being

Thesaurus: Word Journeys // Jennifer Guyor Jowett

stranach

within the sea cove
water murmurations
draw in and pull out

grimlins

midsummer night hours fade
imperceptibly
dusk becomes dawn

suthering

the sound of the wind
moving under, within the wings of the swan
and whispering through the trees

kawaakari

the last gleam
upon the river's surface
as light dusks

daalamist

valley mist
gathered in the night
to exhale at dawn

gandferd

spirits depart
calling forth a storm
like a flying coven

Jennifer Guyor Jowett teases stories and writers into being. She is the author of *Into the Shadows,* a middle grade historical fiction based on true-life events, the creator of the #dogearedbookaward, and a defender of fierce girls. Jennifer is a 7th/8th ELA teacher in the mitten state.

Pebbles in My Palm // Jamie Jo Hoang

Dirt in my hand,
pebbles in my palm.
Heritage in Vietnam.
Home is where I am.

Words I know dance on the breeze.
Hoa hồ ng is a rose.
Hoa sen, a lotus.
I speak not with ease.

I sound American because I am American,
but I am also Vietnamese.
So I listen to tradition
passed down in song and dance.
Fans in hands, a spark of imagination.
History at a glance.

With the flick of a wrist
culture is served — up with a twist.
Feel the wind, stand in place,
let it swoosh, let it sway, let it fly across your face.

Dirt in my hand,
pebbles in my palm.
Heritage in Vietnam.
Home is where I am.

Fans close, opening as flowers on the ground
sprouting from seeds that tumble and fall.
Tossed in a turbulent tempest
                    outward bound
blooming everywhere, all year-round.

I am the bud of a new generation,
rooted in old and nurtured by new.
I dance to practice our customs,
to imagine toiling in the soil
and rolling pebbles between my fingers
from a land that nourished my ancestors.

Knowing where I come from
helps me to become
the me I want to be.
And if ever I lose my way,
I will reach for the earth,
press dirt in my hand,
squeeze pebbles in my palm,
think of my heritage in Vietnam,
and remember that home
is where I am.

Jamie Jo Hoang is the daughter of Vietnamese refugees. She grew up in Orange County, CA—not the rich part. She is the author of *My Father, the Panda Killer* and *Blue Sun, Yellow Sky* Her work has also appeared in TIME, SALON and TinyBuddha.

Chase // Sandra Marchetti

As the lightning
jagged across
the sky she
grabbed a bolt
and stuffed it
down her throat.

Sandra Marchetti is the author of two full-length collections of poetry, *Aisle 228* from Stephen F. Austin State University Press (2023) and *Confluence* from Sundress Publications (2015). She is also the author of four chapbooks of poetry and lyric essays. Sandra's poetry and essays appear widely in *Blackbird, Ecotone, Southwest Review, Mid-American Review, Fansided* and elsewhere.

Herencia // Alicia Partnoy

No quiero que veas, no quiero que veas
mi niño pequeño,
el cuerpo en la arena, bañado de brea
del pájaro muerto.

Prefiero asustarte, prefiero asustarte
con otros terrores:
fantasmas de espuma, gigantes que rugen
ocultos dolores.

Quisiera explicarte, mi niño pequeño
que el hombre es culpable
por andar sembrando las playas del mundo
de tanto cadáver.

Cómo confesarte que queda en tus manos
proteger los sueños
del mar y la tierra, de tanto asesino
que se cree su dueño.

La poeta y activista Alicia Partnoy es autora, traductora o editora de doce libros y del cuadernillo Ecos lógicos y otros poemares. Su obra ha sido publicada en castellano, inglés, francés, turco, bengalí y hebreo. Es más conocida por *La Escuelita. Relatos Testimoniales* sobre su experiencia como desaparecida en los años setenta en Argentina. Partnoy es profesora emérita de la Universidad Loyola Marymount de Los Ángeles.

Inheritance // Alicia Partnoy
(Translated by Julia Horton)

I don't want you to see, I don't want you to see,
dear little boy,
the corpse of that bird, bathed in tar,
lying on the sand.

I'd rather scare you, I'd rather scare you
with other terrors:
phantoms made of foam, giants who bellow
secret sufferings.

Oh how I want to explain, dear little boy
that mankind is guilty
for all those dead bodies
sown in the sand all over the world.

It's so hard to confess that the burden is yours
to defend the dreams
of the sea and the shore from every murderer
who asserts he's their master.

Poet and human rights activist Alicia Partnoy is the author, translator or editor of twelve books and the chapbook *Ecos lógicos y otros poemares*. Her work is published in Spanish, English, Hebrew, Turkish, Bangla, and French. Partnoy is best known for *The Little School: Tales of Disappearance and Survival*, about her experience as a "disappeared" in Argentina in the 70's. Partnoy is Professor Emerita at Loyola Marymount University in Los Angeles.

The Queen of Bees // Kacie Day

In the warmth of spring she'd sit in the valley
Humming her lively tune
As she'd sway, the creatures would sashay,
And they'd pray for the fruits of June
She would breathe in deep and breathe out life
All in time with circadian rhythm
Workers would bow down, revered her crown
They knew she was stronger with them
Together they'd fly all through the night
Giving hope to the world surrounding
All whom they'd pass, would tip their hats
With gratitude and admiration abounding

But

As years went by, we forgot those who fly
And stopped taking time to aid their endeavors
The flowers now die, and with their demise
The bees cannot fly whatsoever
And when the bees slow, and hide from the cold
Queen bee cannot keep up the fight
A millennium pact, careful balancing act,
Now faded in cool morning light
If Queen bee is laid to rest, upon great Earth's breast
The world as we know it is at stake
For when the Queen of Bees dies, we'll all realize
We must give in order to take.

Kacie Day is a rising poet and author whose work explores the beauty and challenges of the human experience. She resides in rural North Dakota with her husband and son, finding inspiration in nature and her close-knit community.

Witness // Sandra Marchetti

A fat snake
swiveled down
a branch
into the river
and I wondered,
what if I had
missed that?
I said to a
girl, "They're
usually not
that big,"
sure she had
seen it flop,
but she said
"Thank God
I did not.
I would have
screamed
bloody murder!"
I walked on
smiling, tracing
the thing's
path, its
inevitable
disappearance.

Sandra Marchetti is the author of two full-length collections of poetry, *Aisle 228* from Stephen F. Austin State University Press (2023) and *Confluence* from Sundress Publications (2015). She is also the author of four chapbooks of poetry and lyric essays. Sandra's poetry and essays appear widely in *Blackbird, Ecotone, Southwest Review, Mid-American Review, Fansided* and elsewhere.

Erased // Erin Murphy

an erasure created from the text of a July 3, 2021
Washington Post *article on the planned*
demolition of the collapsed Champlain Towers
condominium in Surfside, Florida

What is left is fragile.
Wind, rain, and fire

move faster. A cost
is coming to the coast —

flooding, wreckage, disaster.
Can we make revisions

to a month, a day,
a morning — collapse

time, the need to be
in motion? Hope,

memory, everyone
we know — that is

what's left, what's left
to implode.

Originally published in *Ecotone*, March 2023. Reprinted with permission of the author.

Erin's Murphy's work has appeared in *The Best of Brevity, Ecotone, The Georgia Review, Rattle, Women's Studies Quarterly,* and elsewhere. She is the author or editor of more than a dozen books, most recently *Fluent in Blue* (Grayson Books). She is professor of English at Penn State Altoona. **www.erin-murphy.com**

Jibaro Dreams // Emanuel Xavier

En la isla de Nueva York
I search for secret gardens
spiritual sanctuaries
a child lost in a forest of *Jibaro* dreams
where *santos* sail through the *salsa* of my soul
& only fruits fallen from the tree
violently smashing against once rat-infested grounds
remind me of the outside world
sweet juices spilling feeding
the soil
with *abuelas lagrimas*
fathering life to our culture
nature to our concrete jungle
Earth bathing in virgin nectars
lodging seeds in uncemented wombs
struggling for growth somewhere beneath
the choking tight clothes of buildings and overpopulation
outside verandah fortresses
Spanish lullabies and *guaguanco* healing her birth
amongst the casitas *de nuestra gente*
still standing defiantly
freedom from oppression paradise
amidst metal and decay

Emanuel Xavier is author of several poetry books including *Selected Poems of Emanuel Xavier* and *Love(ly) Child*. His books have been finalists for International Latino Book Awards and Lambda Literary Awards and his work has appeared in Poetry, A Gathering of the Tribes, Best American Poetry, and elsewhere.

(Mapping: A Key) // Jennifer Guyor Jowett

Fairy Tale Guidebook
mapping

When wolves come lurking
near woods
long
lost
asking directions, recipes to
soothe hunger
When winds arrive
big
bad
causing straw, sticks to blow
and houses tumble down
When rain falls
beneath a sky
bone
dry
leaving behind, below
the river's maw
When apples offer
red
delicious
promises of eternal
eternalness
That is when the clock
midnights
and godmothers grant wishes
to those who arrive
brandishing
the strength of who they are
and the wisdom to turn fairy tales
into legends

Jennifer Guyor Jowett teases stories and writers into being. She is the author of *Into the Shadows,* a middle grade historical fiction based on true-life events, the creator of the #dogearedbookaward, and a defender of fierce girls. Jennifer is a 7th/8th ELA teacher in the mitten state.

La abuela y el mar // Alicia Partnoy

Pasaban dos gigantes por la playa
marcando sus patazas en la arena.

Navegaban pescadores en barcazas
llevándose el mar para la cena.

Seis delfines cabalgaban en las olas,
carne del agua, sangre de algún mito.

Quise guardarme el océano en los ojos,
mas sólo me robé un caracolito.

El caracol más perfecto recogí:
el que tenía un agujerito.

Soñé con engarzarlo en un collar
para mis corazones de alelí.

La poeta y activista Alicia Partnoy es autora, traductora o editora de doce libros y del cuadernillo Ecos lógicos y otros poemares. Su obra ha sido publicada en castellano, inglés, francés, turco, bengalí y hebreo. Es más conocida por *La Escuelita. Relatos Testimoniales* sobre su experiencia como desaparecida en los años setenta en Argentina. Partnoy es profesora emérita de la Universidad Loyola Marymount de Los Ángeles.

The Grandmother and the Sea // Alicia Partnoy
(Translated by Julia Horton)

Two giants traversed the seashore,
stamping the sand with their footprints.

Fishermen sailed in their sizeable boats,
carrying with them the sea for supper.

Six dolphins glided over the waves,
flesh of the water, blood of a myth.

I wanted my eyes to stow away the sea,
yet all I stole were three little shells.

I picked them up: the most perfect shells,
the ones that had small holes in them–

I dreamed of turning them into pendants
to rest on your hearts, my three sweetie pies.

Poet and human rights activist Alicia Partnoy is the author, translator or editor of twelve books and the chapbook Ecos lógicos y otros poemares. Her work is published in Spanish, English, Hebrew, Turkish, Bangla, and French. Partnoy is best known for *The Little School: Tales of Disappearance and Survival,* about her experience as a "disappeared" in Argentina in the 70's. Partnoy is Professor Emerita at Loyola Marymount University in Los Angeles.

Just
essays

love land world futures being

Living Near St. Catherine School // Jonathon Medeiros

I don't recall the question or the response I gave, but I remember the frustration rising in the nun's face, creeping up her neck before turning her mottled brown cheeks dark purple. She asked again, her words clipped, her lips tight, her long black habit shivering with her consternation, as the class nervously giggled. And another response from me, possibly the same response. I don't remember saying the wrong thing on purpose. I wasn't trying to be smart or funny. There was clearly a gap between Sister Scholastica's query and my understanding of her desires, a gap that distressed me as I watched it yawn open---

She grabbed one of those over large chalkboard erasers from behind her and threw it at me.

"Tssst! Joanahton!"

I ducked and the eraser clattered across the floor. The class was silent for a moment before a loud guffaw snapped the air.

She grunted, reached back behind her again, maybe embarrassed that she missed or maybe angry at Kama's laughter. Her searching hand found the teacher's edition of the social studies book. This she hurled with two hands and an audible, guttural effort. Kama ducked and the book hit someone else squarely in the face.

I can't imagine this did not break that student's nose but I can't recall the immediate aftermath. I don't remember blood or crying or Sister Scholastica being in trouble or even being embarrassed by her anger at children.

Later, some other day, maybe during the uncomfortable week when the nuns taught us about where children come from, I remember listening to Sara cry from the broom closet, its door locked tight inches behind my head. I wonder what Sister Scholastica would say now that Sara is out of that closet and all the others.

I live just a few tenths of a mile from the school now, up on a hill over town. Every Sunday I hear the bells ring and it is a pleasant sound. But as the chimes roll over the treetops like the church itself breathing out a sigh and a prayer, if I think of anything, I think of that book flying across the room, I think of the sound of Sara crying, I think of Alma telling me I had nice shoes and how Sandra always talked to me at lunch and how strange it is to miss a friend you haven't seen in 30 years because you will never see her again.

I remember the volcano we built, the way I broke my front tooth on the monkey bars or the time I had no money for lunch, so I sat in the classroom with one of the nuns. I sometimes remember the line of cactus behind the cafeteria, the time the invisible spines irritated my hands for days, or the hard ice we bought from Mother Superior's office at the end of the day on Fridays.

I remember the time an 8th grader told me to stand against the wall in the bathroom and so I did, my corduroy pants hot on my legs. The way the tile felt cool against my back even through my undershirt and button up. The sound of his feet as he ran across the room and kneed me full speed in my crotch. The way I bent over in pain but didn't make a sound and how his laughter turned to some kind of an apology about how he thought I might move. I remember also the time I wasn't allowed to go to the bathroom or maybe I didn't ask to go out of worry and so I sat in my own urine soaked seat, hoping no one would notice, hoping it would dry while everyone else had recess. The nun did not speak to me as I sat there alone. She must have known, right?

The school is still basically the same as it was: two long buildings, parallel, with a courtyard in between. I remember needing to look for Maile every morning, after the all school prayer in the yard. She was in 7th and 8th grades when I was in 1st and 2nd, I think. She was tall and her hair was thick and black, like a crashing wave of ink roaring off of her head, framing her long nose and dark eyes, her smile, a flower always right there behind her ear. Always. I loved to look for her and watch her walk away, to see her impossible hair almost touching the ground as she strode, barefoot, back to her class, around the corner in the other building.

Sometimes when I go to the bank in Kapaʻa I think I see Alma, from that day in kindergarten. I see flashes of these people, 5 year olds, 4th graders, former teachers, first crushes, youthful tormentors, briefly dancing behind the eyes and smiles of the people who walk by me in my present life.

Isn't that you, Ms. Kaye? I think as I drop my daughter off at daycare and wonder about time folding over on itself, the past touching other moments across our timelines.

I don't ask or confirm when I see these ghosts in the faces of the present. I just let the memories visit, passing me like the sounds of the bells on Sunday, like the scent of plumeria on the breeze, like the crunch of ice between my teeth as I walk up a hill under the sun, like a woman walking on the path, her long hair trailing down, like the smell of urine in a hot restroom, like the sound of a book hitting the floor.

Jonathon Medeiros, former director of the Kauaʻi Teacher Fellowship, has been teaching and learning about Language Arts and rhetoric for nearly 20 years with students on Kauaʻi and he frequently writes about education, equity, and the power of curiosity. He believes in teaching his students that if you change all of your mistakes and regrets, you'd erase yourself. Many of his poems and essays can be found at jonathonmedeiros.com. Reach out at jonathonmedeiros@gmail.com.

Stupid Girls // Jen Ferguson

ONE

To collect our lost things, Forest drove us along the abandoned railway—the rain slowed, the lake calmed—and while Forest drove, he flirted, and teased us for not being *stupid girls*, and still that's what I remember most, not the portages that hadn't been cleared of freefall or the interior of the park wild and quiet, but how things always seemed more serious in the rain, and how Forest, older than us by a year or two, how he admired the stupid girls he wished we were.

TWO

Before our unplanned hike, before the rain, we laid in our two-person tent and I told stories about the bear who killed, maimed boys years back on this very lake, about how when I sleep in Algonquin Provincial Park, I always think of windigo, white-washed and safe on TV.

THREE

Crushing loose gravel pilled along the tracks, we dreamed out loud of penne all'arrabbiata, unlimited breadsticks from that fast food Italian place. Carbs would warm us. When we found the cabins, old enough that they predated the parklands, first we knocked on doors, our teeth chattering.

FOUR

All this cottage country was locked up tight.

"They're gone for the season," my best friend said.

I nodded toward a window. "Should we... ?"

"If we get inside, we'll leave a note."

FIVE

Once we met a grizzled man who lived inside the boundaries, who named his son Forest, as if this wasn't too pointed. Once after a series of late August thunderstorms drove the moose into hiding, my fingers cramped around my paddle until I couldn't unclench them. Once we left our rented canoe in the brush along old train tracks like we were writing a bad nature poem.

Jen Ferguson is Métis with ancestral ties to the Red River and white, an activist, a feminist, an auntie, and an accomplice armed with a PhD. She is the award-winning (and award-losing!) author of *The Summer of Bitter and Sweet*, *Those Pink Mountain Nights* and *A Constellation of Minor Bears*.

Swinging // Karen J. Weyant

The grape vines in the woods were the best kinds of swings.

They were better than our old tires knotted with thick rope to tree branches. Too heavy for any real movement, we had to be pushed by someone in order to gain momentum. Plus, there was always the threat that the branch carrying both the weight of the tire and a child would snap. They were never truly comfortable, and hot days were the worst: where our legs curled around the knotted tie, rubber burned our bare thighs. Sometimes, newer tires that still had thread, left marks.

They were even better than the "real swings" in our neighborhood playgrounds. These swings were made of flat wooden boards and thick chains that rusted, staining our hands when we held tight. Yes, sometimes, we would pump high, pushing our whole bodies forward while trying to pretend that we could fly, but mostly, we sat still and slowly twirled around and around and around, until we let go, spinning in circles until we grew dizzy.

Our grape vines wrapped around tree trunks and branches, so tight, that we had to yank them free. Still, the tug of war was worth the effort, as the vines never broke under our play. They were more than just swings, as they helped us dangle from branches or climb ragged tree trunks. Our hands, already calloused from chain swings or hot rubber, never minded the rough vines.

What we didn't know then but now have to consider is that they may not have been grape vines, but some kind of invasive species that were originally used for aesthetic purposes around homes. The plant quickly escaped into forested areas, including our beloved Pennsylvania woods.

What we didn't know was what we loved so much, what we fought to tug free for our own play, actually killed the trees, the vines thickening and slowly wrapping around them until they cut deep into the bark, until they smothered them.

We didn't know that something we loved could do so much damage to the world around us.

Karen J. Weyant's first full-length collection, *Avoiding the Rapture* was published last fall by Riot in Your Throat press. Her poems have appeared in *Crab Orchard Review*, *Copper Nickel*, *Harpur Palate*, *Fourth River*, *Lake Effect*, *Rattle*, *River Styx* and *Slipstream*. She lives, reads and writes in Northern Pennsylvania but is an Associate Professor of English at Jamestown Community College in Jamestown, New York.

Just
fiction

love land world futures being

Lights Out // Brittany Saulnier

I tap my pencil eraser against my textbook. I gave up on it a while ago. When the clock says it's time, I snap off my desk lamp.

Tonight is a good night, tonight is a chance to breathe, tonight is my favorite holiday, even if nobody has any idea what I'm talking about, even if my friend Lena says it's just something my mom made up, and even if that kid that sits behind us in class sneers that it's because my family is poor.

The other lights upstairs are already off. Candlelight flickers up the stairwell.

Mom didn't make it up. She didn't set the time or date, but when I was a baby, she *did* cast a spell of magic over the night, just like she does for all holidays.

I follow the candlelight down to our living room. Wrapped around the banister is a gold, twisty streamer with silver stars that probably was meant for a New Year's Eve party. The paper was pretty in the daytime but now it sparkles in the low light.

Mom and Dad sit together on the sofa. My sister Jillian kneels on the floor beside the coffee table. When she sees me coming down the stairs, she bounces on her knees.

"I won!" she beams.

"By default!" I tease. "We could have switched math homework and then seen who was done first!"

"Come on girls! Ready?" Dad asks. He smiles wide as Jillian poises over the tray of mismatched candles collected from every corner of the house, and then looking down at his watch, he leads the countdown, "5..., 4..., 3..., 2..., 1!"

Julian blows away the light.

The house is wonderfully dark, except for the white light from the neighbor's garage illuminating the kitchen window and it's like I'm a fish, held by the dark expansive ocean, looking up, perplexed, at a wayward ship's navigation lights.

Silently, Dad leads the way out the back door. Mom has already put blankets and beach towels on our small square of lawn. She set up the telescope and filled each of our baskets with goodies, too. I get a new canvas bag with a pretty flower design and a matching journal made from recycled paper. My sister gets seed packets and a book about bugs. And of course, we both have star shaped cookies.

After we peek through the baskets, and mouth a silent *thank you* to Mom, my sister and I stretch out on the beach towels. I clasp one hand in hers and then press the other gently into the grass.

I look up at the gray night sky and try to see all of it at once, as far as I can. I search for the Big Dipper.

But my gaze is averted by a flash of light to the side and I'm pulled out of the spell. Mrs. Carter peeks from behind her curtain at us and then dashes away inside her bright home.

We've lived next to Mrs. Carter for years and she still looks out at us and gasps. Does she also think that the only reason to sit outside in the dark is because the electric company turned off all the lights? Oh, the poor children on the ground!

I squeeze my sister's hand and turn back to the deep, expansive night waiting above me. The world slips away, all of it, and I'm no longer a fish but a star, steady, maybe even stoic, in the haze.

Although impossible, space *darkens.*

My body takes over my daydreams, jolting me upright just in time.

One by one my neighbors' houses go dark.

All down the street.

I hear Mrs. Carter's slow steps moving over her wooden deck, the creaks loud in the stillness.

Then the street lamps go black. I didn't think that was possible. What about the crime? Or the late commuters?

My sister tightens her grip on my hand so I follow her gaze.

We watch Mom reach over the fence.

She hands Mrs. Carter a basket.

"Thank you," Mrs. Carter says too loudly. She winces and whispers, "Sorry! I'm a little nervous."

Mrs. Carter eases herself down into her Adirondack chair and leans her head back.

I lay down, again, and try to let the world drift away, again, expecting to drift into maybe a deeper, darker void of space, but this time seven stars shine down at me, connected only by imaginary lines.

I realize I am not only a star, I'm a star in a constellation.

Brittany Saulnier is on a quest to inspire readers to find their own connection to nature. She is inspired by nature's secrecy and often blends environmental science with whimsy. Her short stories have been longlisted for anthologies and competitions. In addition to writing, Brittany co-created the *Read to Write Kidlit Podcast*.

The Stillness of Flight // David Schaafsma

When Greg found the dead sparrow on the sidewalk in front of his house he stopped, knelt on both knees and paused, waiting for it to spring to life. Setting his backpack down, he closed his eyes, shut them tight, and pressed the heels of his palms hard against his thighs. He moved as slowly and as little as possible. He willed the bird to move; he opened his eyes and watched the small breast for breath. He poked it gently with his forefinger, nudging it with his knuckle. Nothing.

After a few moments, resigned, he cupped the bird with his two hands, raised it up as if it were a delicate flower, and carried it behind his garage. With his fingers and then a pen from his backpack he scratched at the cold November topsoil, dug the grave a little more than a fistful deep, and pressed the soil over the bird with his palms. When he returned to pick up his backpack, he noticed his mother watching him from the kitchen window as he approached the house. She was expecting him home, after school. He didn't acknowledge her, looked away, and shuffled to the back door, rubbing the dirt from his hands.

Greg slid, fully clothed, under the covers of his bed, and lay as flat as possible on his stomach. He lay very still. He shut his eyes tight and tried very hard not to think of anything. This was always impossible, of course; honking horns from the street, or his mother's insistent call to supper, always these intrusions. But in recent months he had been making a serious attempt, anyway, each day after school. Many times since last spring he had not gone to school, huddling under the sheets in his bed, behind his tightly closed door.

He ached to stop up his eyes, his ears, the nerve endings lying close under his skin, and to slow the steady pounding of the blood in his brain. If he lay very still he could imagine the shrinking going on: The lump of himself under the blanket, like dough set to rise, seemed to be gradually deflating, as if it had been disrupted by a sudden jolt, losing shape and form, no longer to rise. He had the will-power to do it, he was confident of that. Even now, he could almost shut it all out.

It was his mother who had encouraged him to explore birds, seeing his initial interest. She helped him identify different birds in the neighborhood. She helped him choose books from the library on birds of the midwest. He began to study their various songs, their flight patterns, their differences.

The floating of wings on air, seemingly so effortless, was really stillness, Greg thought; it was the illusion of motion to mere humans craning their necks from the ground. Inside, the birds were still, Greg knew. He watched them rise and dive, he admired their quick, darting escapes and their tremendous explosive power, and yet, he knew, they were somehow still.

From the gradual slope of his roof he had often watched the birds resting in the great dark oak tree in the side yard next to his house. From the edge of the roof he felt he could almost touch them. Sometimes he stretched out a hand as if to measure the distance that separated him from the nearest tip of the nearest branch. Less than fifteen feet away, a branch sturdy enough to bear his weight reached out to him.

The drop between the room and the branch was over two stories to the concrete driveway that separated the house from the yard. Imagining that leap nearly froze him with fear and delight. The skittish birds sometimes watched him warily, hopping from branch to branch. He sat as quietly as possible, motionless, so they might trust him. Each day he felt closer to them. When the birds flew, dark flecks against the blue sky, darting explosions of fluttering motion, Greg would watch them, imagine himself soaring with them as far as he could see them fly.

He opened the door to the back porch and noticed it was getting late. It must be nearly nine, he thought. He observed the light of the pale moon rising, and the fainter, surrounding stars. He took a deep breath, steadied his feet on the ladder, gripped the rungs firmly and hoisted himself up on the roof. How could any-- merely human--beings, know what it meant to fly?

Greg stood firmly on the roof and tested his weight on the edge, to determine how much it would give if he thrust out from it. He paced a few feet back from the edge, bending his knees several times, bouncing on his toes, flexing his arms, twisting his shoulders, arching his back, an acrobat poised for the swing. He found it difficult to steady himself. He trembled a little, feeling sweat crawl down the back of his neck.

He tried to shut it all out. All of it. He shut his eyes tight and used all the will-power he could summon. But then he thought of the bird, the sparrow he had buried. He sat down and hugged his knees. He thought how it was that the bird may have died. The horrifying crash, the end of it all. And he opened his eyes. He went inside, trying to decide what to do.

And then he saw the bird seed package his mother must have left out for him. He sat on his bed, considering. He got up and walked out to the roof again. He opened the package and began to scatter seeds all around him, as far as he could reach, with both hands, and sat down, putting some seed in both hands, his arms outstretched, closing his eyes. Maybe this was better. He heard a goldfinch to his left come close to the roof and fly to a tree nearby. He sat as still as he could and waited.

David Schaafsma is a Professor of English at the University of Illinois at Chicago where he directs the Program in English Education. He teaches courses in English teaching methods, and literature. He's the author or co-editor of six books and is in the process of writing more.

The Listener // Aimee Parkison

Behind the broken rails of the white fence, she moved, startling the deer. Near the cattails, she fed scraps to the dogs tied to the east wall near her sister's face at the window, sweet breath fogging smudged glass. Every spring, the pond encroached upon the house after the rains, deer drinking from its murky edge where paint flecks floated, breaking apart on bark, leaves, and bottles filled with air. Styrofoam clashed with embers in the wind's wake, the cup torn apart. The dogs swam under their leashes to chase bits of biscuit floating out the door to the water. Mayflies skimmed the surface and clung to the window screens. As she watched the wings' shadow cross her sister's face, she didn't have anything to say. Even when she left the house, she would not speak to her brother in words. From her sister to her mother to her father's sun-darkened hands, vases, coffee cups, sugar cubes, and teaspoons were dried and exchanged in silence. Watching the dogs at the window, she often became confused and used her mouth for the wrong reasons. Her teeth were like her hands, another way to grasp and carry necessary items from the rooms to the windows and back. Venturing out into the half-immersed porch to sit on the swing in sunlight, she let her feet move in and out of the pond water. Crouching low as she swung, she amused her sister inside, feeding the dogs bread from her mouth. They leapt up to her lips delicately as in a kiss. Their paws splashed back into the water as they carried the bread away, quickly so that the others wouldn't steal the crumbs. Fingers were a last resort. Her sister didn't trust them to touch faces as she trusted a mouth no longer used for speaking. Stumbling toward the window, she pressed her face against the screen to feel the mayflies lighting on her cheek. Sometimes her hands like the deer could be forgotten even by the ones who waited for their return.

Aimee Parkison has published eight books and won FC2's Catherine Doctorow Innovative Fiction Prize and *North American Review's* Kurt Vonnegut Prize. She is Professor of Fiction Writing at OSU. Her work has appeared in *North American Review, Puerto Del Sol, Five Points,* and *Best Small Fictions.* www.aimeeparkison.com

Just World

poetry· flash fiction · essays

Just
poetry

love land world futures being

Moonscape // Zetta Elliott

today a reporter described what's left of Gaza
as a "moonscape" and I wondered,
what moon looks like this?
I see no craters, no frozen seas
just chalky limbs dangling between
slabs of concrete that once were
ceilings and floors holding space for life
homes for countless families now
turned into tombs for thousands of
children who never knew lunar lightness
only the gravity of living in a prison
designed to destroy
dignity

Zetta Elliott's poetry has been published in numerous anthologies. Her first YA collection, *Say Her Name*, won the 2021 Lion and the Unicorn Award for Excellence in North American Poetry. *A Place Inside of Me: A Poem to Heal the Heart* was named a 2021 Notable Poetry Book by the NCTE.

Juneteenth is Not Freedom // Stacey Joy

Wondering
if I
am really free

To
be Black
and proud me

I'm
still denied
my total freedom

To
be Black
in white america

Juneteenth
can't free
the wrongfully incarcerated

Juneteenth
can't free
the enslaved mind

Does
america hear
caged birds sing?

Stacey Joy is a National Board Certified Teacher who has taught for 38 years in Los Angeles. Stacey is a self-published poet and has poems published in various anthologies: *Out of Anonymity, Savant Poetry Anthologies, Teacher Poets Writing to Bridge the Distance*, and *Rhythm and Rhyme: Poems for Student Athletes.*

Girls' Playground, Harriet Island, St. Paul, MN (1905) // Jennifer Guyor Jowett

We were young adventurers
Climbers
Swingers
Risk takers
The fuss and prim
did not prevent us from reaching
places unexpected.
Our faces full of determination
and spunk,
we watched as one or two,
the first of us,
moved beyond the earth's hold,
testing the boundaries of gravity,
pulling from inner strength and
proving what we all knew we could do.
We had stars in our eyes
A handhold on the future
Saw glimpses of what could be
And latched on.

Jennifer Guyor Jowett teases stories and writers into being. She is the author of *Into the Shadows,* a middle grade historical fiction based on true-life events, the creator of the #dogearedbookaward, and a defender of fierce girls. Jennifer is a 7th/8th ELA teacher in the mitten state.

Belonging // Joe Bisicchia

So much is to believing,
we are all
of a kind.

One by one by
everyone.

There is a house on the hill,
and in the valley,
and on a mountain,
and in the desert,
and on the water,
and in the forest,
and in the jungle,
and on the white tundra,
and within the elevated city,
and everywhere, same
of a kind.

The world is such a house.

And at heart of house,
find an embraced *us*.
The difference
between an address
and more importantly
home.

What a gift to belong.
Treasure box of our own.

Joe Bisicchia has nearly four decades of experience in language arts, from journalism and broadcasting, to teaching, marketing, public affairs, and poetry. An Honorable Mention recipient for the Fernando Rielo XXXII World Prize for Mystical Poetry, he has written four published collections of poetry.

We Gather Here Together // Rachel Toalson

It's hard not to notice
the vultures gathering

they're not inconspicuous at all
against the gray sky, slate pavement

they're opportunistic
waiting for the fall

and every time I try
to ignore them

one calls out, Hey, baby
I'll take you home if you need a ride

I don't dignify the comment
with attention

I'm not out here for them
as much as they'd like to believe I am

I am my own private
gathering

I'm out here for
all the women in me

*This poem first appeared in Here: a poetry journal.

Rachel Toalson is the author of *The Colors of the Rain*, *The Woods*, *The First Magnificent Summer*, and *Something Maybe Magnificent* (Simon & Schuster, 2024). Her poetry has been published in print magazines and literary journals around the world. She lives in San Antonio, Texas, with her husband and six sons.

Just Word(le) // **Jennifer Guyor Jowett**

/jə st/

> behaving according to what is right and morally fair
> "a just and equitable world"

T U O R T

in a world
where they want us to make-believe
and look the other way,
pretend we didn't see
what took place before us,
we hold this to be self-evident

R M H Y T

within a yellowed wood
the choice to explore the road,
downtrodden or otherwise,
can not matter –
existence belongs to everyone

I R E D E

belief in a world
where we value
humanity in the human
justice in the just
where principle is principal
and life is for living

Q U A I L

we can math our way
divide and subtract
to infinity
but this sum is infinite

H Y O O R

set fire to both heart and words
carry the integrity of our grandmothers
the merit of our grandfathers
who trod upon this dirt
and rise (we must not be moved)

W O R L D

we live in our truth
where right is a creed
and equal an honor

Family Stories // Mary E. Cronin

~after Emma Lazarus

You keep telling these old family stories — give
me a break. They can't *all* be saints. Don't tell me
everyone had perfect immigration papers in your
family tree. This noble narrative — it's tired.
Are you really sure that your
relatives were so perfect? They were poor,
yes, and scrappy. Maybe they had *no* papers, your
ancestors! Now you all watch the news, huddled
together, saying that *outsiders* are coming in masses.
You talk about the old days with a yearning.
But who knows if your people — our family — came to
this country "the right way?" They just want to breathe,
these newcomers. Like us, they just want to be free.

"The golden shovel is a poetic form wherein each word of one line
from another poem serves as the end word of each line for a newly
constructed poem" (Poets.org, from the American Academy of
Poets).

Mary E. Cronin is a poet, author, and Literacy Coach who lives on
Cape Cod in Massachusetts. Her picture book biography of PFLAG
founder Jeanne Manford, LIKE A MOTHER BEAR, is forthcoming
from Simon & Schuster/Atheneum. Her poetry has been featured
in *The New York Times, Radical Teacher, Rise Up Review*, and in *Rhyme
and Rhythm: Poems for Student Athletes.* She is represented by Lori
Steel of SteelWorks Literary. You can reach her at
www.maryecronin.com.

There Must Be a Gate // Laura Shovan

Where there is a wall
there must be a gate,
a way to enter the garden
on the other side.

Birds need no permission
to migrate overhead.
Moles tunnel the earth
to get through.

For them, brick and concrete
are inconsequential.
Barbed wire,
a human concern.

We must pass through the gap --
if one exists -- wingless,
clawless, on the same two feet
that carried us days

and miles to reach this wall.
Identity vouchers
and proof
of public education

are sewn into our pockets.
There must be a gate,
We tell ourselves.
We have seen this wall before.

Laura Shovan is a Pushcart Prize nominated poet and a middle grade novelist. Among her award-winning children's books are *The Last Fifth Grade of Emerson Elementary*, *Takedown*, and *A Place at the Table*, written with Saadia Faruqi. Laura is a longtime poet-in-the-schools. She teaches at Vermont College of Fine Arts.

I Refuse to Be Underestimated // Rachel Toalson

They used to think
we didn't have a brain

Some still believe it—
not that they'd admit it

They water down the bias
make it more palatable—
our brains were not meant for
    science
    technology
    math
    engineering
    mechanics
    the great works of literary merit
Try to keep up, sweetie, they say
It's complicated, I know

One of life's greatest frustrations
is being underestimated

One of life's greatest tragedies
is learning to underestimate ourselves
because of someone else's
ignorance

Rachel Toalson is the author of *The Colors of the Rain*, *The Woods*, *The First Magnificent Summer*, and *Something Maybe Magnificent* (Simon & Schuster, 2024). Her poetry has been published in print magazines and literary journals around the world. She lives in San Antonio, Texas, with her husband and six sons.

Unconstitutional // Stacey Joy

Crave unity
The perfect kind
A union
Of differences
Celebrated and honored
Respected and preserved

Seek justice
For all human kind
Indivisible
Equitable
No hands up
And we will breathe

Pursue tranquility
With hoodies on
While jogging
When driving
Where standing
While being Black

Demand defense
Protection from enemies
Within white houses
Behind blue codes
Across every street
Inside cold courtrooms

Destroy poverty
Dismantle systemic racism
Secure all liberties
To live fearless
With radical love
For ourselves and our posterity

Stacey Joy is a National Board Certified Teacher who has taught for 38 years in Los Angeles.

Peace Play // Linda Mitchell

The people grew weary of war
and the sadness of war
and all its destruction
when someone said,
Let's play peace, now.

And the people,
rusty at peace-play
slowly put down their phones
and their pride.

They picked up dice
letter tiles, pawns
or decks of cards–
dusting them off and dealing
until every person
in World's every corner
had a new hand.

Placing pairs on the table
drawing new cards from the deck
taking turns
talking about their days
talking and chuckling
forgetting who
won the last round
anyway.

Linda Mitchell is a family girl, school librarian and creative person. She hangs out with her laptop, scissors, glue and paper from discarded books to make crafts with two mischievous young cats. Her favorite game is cribbage. She has published in several journals and weekly to her Poetry Friday blog, *A Word Edgewise.*

Just essays

love   land   world   futures   being

Irish Whistle // Kate Sjostrom

I've never felt so old and so young at the same time: Friday night in a bona fide nightclub. It's an all-ages show, which lessens my esteem for the club, but we seem to be the only high schoolers here, which takes the place back up a notch. Even so, I'm not sold on China Club, which exudes—through its indirect red lighting and "Dragon Room" (off limits to us kids)—a vague colonialism, just the thing Sean tells me the band we're here to see protests.

As Sean told it on the drive downtown, though, there's nothing vague about the way the British oppressed the Irish. I was embarrassed by how little I knew of Irish history, despite being of mostly Irish heritage, and how little I knew of Sean's fervor for it, despite having been in his orbit since fourth grade, when he and I sat at the same table in Mrs. Rossi's homeroom. I cut myself some slack, guessing he wasn't reading biographies of Irish revolutionaries back when we were nine. His is new knowledge, but his resultant anger feels long and deep. "The Troubles aren't over," he told us, turning briefly from the steering wheel. And I wanted to care about those troubles more than I cared about whether Mike was watching me from the burgundy back seat of the Fitzgerald family minivan.

There's no chance we'll blend in here at the club, so I try not to care. Sean doesn't; he's too pumped to see his new favorite frontman from Ireland by way of the Bronx. Mike doesn't seem to care about anything, which I wish wouldn't make him so attractive. He's younger than me and already has a smoker's cough. I know he likes me—Sean told me when he invited me to join them—but you wouldn't guess it from looking at him, which keeps me looking.

Sean has moved us even closer to the stage, so that when the band barrels onto it we're so close I flinch. Just as quickly, I fix on the singer who bangs his head to the bass drum beat that signals serious business. He has red hair and glasses, just like it says in the lyrics to their one song that gets radio play, and I try to place him in my family heritage, try to find traits of brother, father, cousins, uncles in him. His flop of copper hair might be like my dad's was before it settled into auburn age. I don't know. I can't find a definitive connection.

Irish whistle joins the drums and it sounds almost silly to me, making me feel again like a horrible excuse for an Irish person. I try to see into a cloudy memory of going to hear a family friend's band at the Kilkenny Castle Inn, try to attach my parents' interest and approval then to the music in my ears now.

Now the music turns serious again, as the singer takes over to tell of a long-ago uprising against the British. Sean and all the others packed right against the stage raise their fists in solidarity, leaving them up even when the singer lowers his own, leaving them up so long I feel I'm supposed to join in and feel my right hand begin to clench. Still hesitant, I look behind me where the crowd is not nearly as dense, fists rising above it only here and there, then turn to my right where Mike stands, looking right at me.

He gives a small smile and a short laugh that seems to say, "Just what I was thinking," then lifts his hand. But instead of closing his fingers and turning to the stage, he reaches his open hand past me, places its palm on the back of my neck, and pulls me into a kiss. This culture I speak.

We kiss for the rest of the song and all of the next one, not stopping when Sean turns to us in the short silence between songs or when the man next to Mike jokingly offers him a Mentos mint, not stopping until the singer launches into the song we know from the radio, the one we can sing along to.

Kate Sjostrom is a writer and writing teacher educator based in Oak Park, IL. Her work has been published in *Rhyme & Rhythm: Poems for Student Athletes*, RHINO, *English Journal,* and elsewhere.

Just
fiction

love land world futures being

Feathers // Valerie Hunter

Tim stood on the train platform, trying to pretend he did this every day. Mum had offered to see him off, but he was fourteen, capable of walking to the station and buying the ticket himself. They'd said their good-byes at home, Dad shaking his hand, Mum and Audrey hugging him tearfully as though he was shipping off instead of spending the summer at his grandparents' farm in Suffolk.

Since the war began last year, it seemed like everyone in Tim's family had found a way to be useful. Dad was too old to join up, but he worked long hours at the munitions factory. Mum and Audrey had joined the Red Cross, rolling bandages and knitting socks. Audrey was even talking about getting a factory job herself once she turned eighteen in October.

Now it was Tim's turn to do his part. His grandparents' hired man had recently joined up, and Tim could surely replace him. He'd grown a lot this year, towering over Mum and Audrey. He was even a smidge taller than Dad, which seemed unfathomable. Sometimes when Tim looked in the mirror, he wasn't sure he knew himself.

His thoughts were interrupted as a girl in a yellow dress strode towards him. She looked around Audrey's age, but while his sister was always a bit rumpled, this girl was neat as a pin and had a confidence that Tim associated with teachers.

She walked up to him and pressed something into his hand, saying, "You ought to be ashamed of yourself, a big strapping lad not yet signed up! Do your duty for your country so you can hold your head up like a man."

She stalked off, and only then did Tim look at what she'd given him.

A white feather.

He'd heard about the feathers, of course. They were given to men who were shirking their duty.

"I'm only fourteen!" he wanted to shout. But the girl was gone.

The train pulled up, and Tim got aboard, still clutching the feather, mind reeling. The girl had taken him for a coward!

Was he? Of course he wasn't nearly old enough to be a soldier, but he was secretly glad about that. Audrey said the war would end long before Tim turned eighteen. When the war first started last summer, she'd said it confidently. Lately her words sounded both hopeful and slightly desperate.

Of course the war would surely be over by 1919, but with each month that passed, it seemed slightly more possible it wouldn't.

Tim tried not to think about it. Some of his classmates couldn't wait to fight, proclaiming they could whup those Germans single-handedly. Matthew Key wished loudly and fervently multiple times that the war would last long enough for him to join up, a wish that appalled Tim.

Surely he should feel appalled. Surely that didn't make him a coward.

The train pulled into another station, picking up more passengers. Someone sat next to Tim. "Your first?"

Tim startled. His seatmate, a young man, was looking at the feather. Tim squeezed his fist shut, but the shaft bit into his palm.

"Sorry," the young man said. "It's none of my business, but you look a little shaken, and I know a bit about white feathers." He motioned to one sticking out of his shirt pocket. "I'm Lawrence, by the way."

"Tim," he mumbled. "I'm only fourteen." He said this last part louder, as though Lawrence was the one accusing him of cowardice.

He waited for Lawrence to insist he couldn't be so young. Strangers had begun to do this frequently, as if they knew Tim's age better than he did. But Lawrence just said, "Those feather-givers tend to think they know everything, even when they don't."

Tim felt a little buoyed by this sympathy. "Have you gotten many feathers?" he asked, uncertain whether he should have.

"I could probably cover a whole chicken with them," Lawrence said.

"You're...That is, don't you..." He trailed off, unsure what he was trying to ask.

"I'm a pacifist," Lawrence supplied.

"Oh." Tim wasn't sure he understood. "You don't want to fight?"

"I don't believe in war."

Tim turned this sentence over in his head. War wasn't like Father Christmas, to be believed in or not. It was real and terrible, blaring daily from the newspaper's headlines.

"If everyone in England felt like that, we'd be ruled by the Germans," Tim said, then felt his face go hot. Aloud, the words sounded as cruel and judgmental as the feather.

"If everyone in the world felt like I did, we could avoid war in the first place," Lawrence offered. "But sadly I'm an outlier."

"Suppose they conscript you?" Tim asked. The newspaper said conscription was coming now that the war was dragging on.

Lawrence sighed. "I'll cross that bridge when it comes. In the meantime, I'm doing my part raising crops. People always need food, especially in wartime."

"You're a farmer?"

"Yes."

Tim told him about going to his grandparents' farm, which led to a lengthy discussion about crops and harvests. Tim had never felt more grown up.

But in the end his gaze traveled back to the feather sticking out of Lawrence's pocket. "Why do you show it off?"

"It's a reminder that no one can make me ashamed of myself or what I believe in. That I know myself, even if no one else does." The train stopped. "Here's where I get off. It was nice meeting you, Tim."

"Likewise," Tim said, shaking Lawrence's hand. He still had the feather in his other hand.

Lawrence nodded at it. "Do you want me to take that for you?"

Tim shook his head. As Lawrence left the train, Tim slipped the feather deep into his pocket. He wasn't as brave as Lawrence, couldn't imagine wearing the feather for the world to see. Still, he liked the idea of keeping it close, a small reminder that he was starting to know himself.

Valerie Hunter teaches high school English and has an MFA in writing for children and young adults from Vermont College of Fine Arts. Her stories and poems have appeared in magazines such as *Cricket*, *Cicada*, and *Paper Lanterns*, and anthologies including *I Sing: The Body* and *Brave New Girls*.

Hunterlore // Dana Claire

There are terrors in the night that have nothing to do with monsters, and I was determined to become one. But first, apparently, I needed to learn to defend myself.

I shifted my weight on the hard wooden bench we'd pushed against the wall, along with the rest of the furniture, to give Liam and Nikki space to spar in the center of the room. The basement had been meticulously transformed from a storage area into a small gym and studio apartment that played home to our Hunterland learning center, for all things monster related.

"Whoa!" My little sister Pepper covered her mouth, bouncing on the edge of the seat beside me as Liam ducked Nikki's wild punch. Nikki staggered when her fist met air instead of bone but smirked anyway. Our simple, small-town Wisconsin lives had changed a few months ago when Liam Hunter, his sister, Jacqueline, and their father, Jack Hunter, showed up to investigate a string of suspicious suicides in my high school. Well, there was also that bit about a vampire nest and my mother turning into a vengeful spirit. That had thrown us for an even bigger loop.

While the Hunter family helped sort it all out, Liam discovered my sister and I had some magical abilities of our own, and Pepper and I had been fast-tracked to join them as hunters of things that go bump in the night.

Which brought us here. Doc, Hunterland's appointed leader and our current instructor, thought watching Liam and Nikki fight would make a good introduction to training. But each punch made me wonder if I'd withstand even a few seconds of a battle with either of them, despite my newfound healer abilities. All three of us were seniors in high school, but they felt years older than me, and watching them bob and weave only added to that experience gap.

Dana Claire is an award-winning author whose stories explore identity, fate, and destiny in the crossroads of romance and adventure. Her love of romantic tension, the supernatural and non-stop action has elicited positive feedback from many readers, as their online reviews reveal her flair for spine-tingling action and unforgettable characters.

Drive-by (In Three Acts) // Jennifer Guyor Jowett

Number One, In the Present

Deep within the walls of Fowler Brothers Bookstore, words scurried along, hushed whispers echoed, and letters roamed.

The small shop, surrounded by concrete and ironworks, slept by itself, living within shadows and tucked into dark corners. Its shades, half drawn behind black awnings like eyelids, preserved the tomes nestled within. A cat lazed in the window, tail flicking a metronome of beats. There was one door for two purposes – coming and going – but it was rarely used, such was the fate of a sleepy store.

Number Two, In the Past

"Won't find me traipsing around the city streets," Emily wrote in sighs, barely able to be heard above the wild night.

Henry confided his thoughts, pen to journal. "What I wouldn't give to follow a wooded trail to the Merrimack." The scent of wild apples and unfurling ferns could just be snatched from the air.

Will said nothing, concentrating on the small blotch of ink left behind by the quill and wondering if the O could be shaped into a Q and what that might do to his metered words.

Dust pulsed across the faint light cast through wavy glass.

Margaret drew photographs from her imaginings, crafted in alphabets clacked into being under fingertips tapping, her lips moved with the letters, forming gray flecked sentences.

Young Mary stitched together monsters, embroidering pieces of herself, her history, upon linen.

Tattooing awareness into the world, A.T. graffitied initials, carefully extracting the I's and leaving the T, an H, U, and finally a G.

Elizabeth fisted words, opening their eyes to Septembers and Junes and every month of every year.

The shop sat in stillness, the quiet that of a tomb, as the writers wrote; the motes of dust stirred only by the cat.

Edgar's heartbeat thumped beneath the floorboards.

Number Three, In the Future

"Dead? Is it dead?" the man demanded, trying to pry open the cover.

The crowd stood, wearing angry words like cloaks.

"Just leave it," a woman muttered, brushing a hand wearily across her jaw. "There's nothing to be done."

Stepping from those gathered, a child veered closer only to be held back, before being pushed behind the wall of adults, their fingers inked in black.

Someone moved to chalk the line.

With nothing more to do, they wandered off, stepping carefully past the outlines littering the sidewalk, letters pooling black against concrete. But the child lingered, reaching to open the lifeless entity, brows furrowed with concentration, lips moving silently, sounding out the numbers, 4 5 1, the letters unrecognizable.

Jennifer Guyor Jowett teases stories and writers into being. She is the author of *Into the Shadows*, a middle grade historical fiction based on true-life events, the creator of the #dogearedbookaward, and a defender of fierce girls. Jennifer is a 7th/8th ELA teacher in the mitten state.

Just Futures

poetry· flash fiction · essays

Just
poetry

love   land   world   futures   being

Chasing the American Dream // Laura Zucca-Scott

I was chasing the American Dream
Wide-eyed girl, tough as nails
My brother and I found a computer near the dumpster
We fixed it and figured out DOS
I wrote my first college application on it
When I got my scholarship my Mom was so proud
I left on a plane
I had no fear then
I was chasing the American Dream
New country, new language, new life
Going back was always just an illusion
I was chasing the American Dream
Now the AI can write essays and poems on its own
Siri can tell me the weather and how to get home
but does not answer when I ask if I am going to be okay
We need each other more than ever
Seeking all the possibilities
I am still chasing the American Dream

Laura Zucca-Scott, Ph.D. is a Professor at Minot State University and an award-winning creative writer. Her works have been published, in English and Italian, in several anthologies including the "Beatitude, 50th Anniversary" Anthology. Laura is also a recurring contributor to the *North Dakota Quarterly*.

We Need Stories // Jennifer Guyor Jowett

Girls have vanquished monsters
since time's beginning

When green-eyed demons
spout barbed words
and gnarled ogres
allude suggestively,
sharp-witted tongues slay
and no-nonsense looks slice
unworthy opponents

We hold our own
following bread crumbs
until the unexpected is well-trod

We open crypts
and bury the jealous words
and the U and I vowels
that set us apart
from One and We

We shine light on truths
holding lanterns
of our past under scorching fires
until our path forward clears

We have swum in our own tears
drunk the saltiness of earth's oceans,
quenching our thirst
to rise above
bowing our heads
only to receive gold,
circular against our chests
and round upon our brows.

These are the stories we know
the ones we need to tell

Jennifer Guyor Jowett teases stories and writers into being. She is the author of Into the Shadows, a middle grade historical fiction based on true-life events, the creator of the #dogearedbookaward, and a defender of fierce girls. Jennifer is a 7th/8th ELA teacher in the mitten state.

Envision // Joe Bisicchia

Anticipate what reality can bring,
and what a being can bring to reality.
Let inner eyes visualize.

Allow the mind to ride,
sense the outfield fence
and the leap above it.

Dream it, want it,
and make that catch inside the mind.
Destiny waits to take place.

Envision so to imagine what can be
so to give life to the very opportunity.
And then, do your best

to again make that catch.

Joe Bisicchia has nearly four decades of experience in language arts, from journalism and broadcasting, to teaching, marketing, public affairs, and poetry. An Honorable Mention recipient for the Fernando Rielo XXXII World Prize for Mystical Poetry, he has written four published collections of poetry.

A Remembrance // Rachel Toalson

Sometimes I forget
that my decisions carry the weight
of generations

Sometimes I forget
that I belong to others
and they belong to me and
we belong to each other

Sometimes I forget
that kindness and love can
take the form of
self-denial and
restraint

Sometimes I forget
that in my pursuit to
save or (accidentally) destroy the planet
I am not alone
but connected to the world's
past present future

Sometimes I forget
that I am human

Rachel Toalson is the author of *The Colors of the Rain, The Woods, The First Magnificent Summer,* and *Something Maybe Magnificent* (Simon & Schuster, 2024). Her poetry has been published in print magazines and literary journals around the world. She lives in San Antonio, Texas, with her husband and six sons.

Illuminated // Erin Murphy

The night of the closest supermoon
in 70 years, I scrolled through Facebook
posts of friends' photos. Peter's was best:
the moon floated above a red barn
in Roaring Spring like an illuminated balloon
without a string. I'm ashamed to say how long
it took me to look outside at the real thing.

Originally published in *Northern Appalachia Review*, March 2022. Reprinted with permission of the author.

Erin Murphy is the author of more than a dozen books, most recently *Fluent in Blue*. This poem is a demi-sonnet, a seven-line form she invented. Her work has appeared in *The Best of Brevity, Ecotone, Women's Studies Quarterly,* and elsewhere. She is professor of English at Penn State Altoona. www.erin-murphy.com

Star Gatherers // Jennifer Guyor Jowett

Say to the fledglings
say to the nestlings
the first-steppers
the plunge-takers
the course-charters
the road-pavers,
"Even if they tell you
the world is flat,
blaze forth,
fall off the edge,
strap yourself
to thermal engines
and electric fireflies.
Live for the tails of comets.
Live for the dust of meteors,
the candy skies.
Gather the stars.

Jennifer Guyor Jowett teases stories and writers into being. She is the author of Into the Shadows, a middle grade historical fiction based on true-life events, the creator of the #dogearedbookaward, and a defender of fierce girls. Jennifer is a 7th/8th ELA teacher in the mitten state.

Word of the day: Techwright // Stefani Boutelier

i write words
they move to the wall
to the masses
i am a techwright
rite of the digital
extension in my hand
right-click here ☐
my text is viral
i'm now
world-renowned
right?

Stefani Boutelier, Ph.D., is an Associate Professor of Education at Aquinas College in Michigan. She teaches courses for pre-service and in-service teachers focused on instructional design, diverse literacy, technology integration, and research methods. Her K-12 teaching was in Southern California prior to moving into teacher preparation.

Don't Call Me A Robot // Laura Shovan

I am a whiz with numbers,
but my head is filled
with thoughts and feelings,
not gears and calculations.
I'm serious. Don't laugh at me.

I am not a robot.

I never fail a test,
but it's not funny when you pretend
there are buttons on my back
that you can push
and shout, "Beep!"

I am not a robot.

Robots don't get angry
when their friends
say something mean. But I do
because I am a regular kid
who is good at math.

And I am not a robot.

Laura Shovan is a Pushcart Prize nominated poet and a middle grade novelist. Among her award-winning children's books are *The Last Fifth Grade of Emerson Elementary*, *Takedown*, and *A Place at the Table*, written with Saadia Faruqi. Laura is a longtime poet-in-the-schools. She teaches at Vermont College of Fine Arts.

For Sale: M1k0 the Robot // Laura Shovan

This smart robot
is forming
artificial intelligence.
Fully programmable!
It scans
your environment.
M1K0 develops its own
gestures and emotions.
Easy
to follow
instructions!

Instructions
to follow?
Easy.
Gestures and emotions?
M1K0 develops its own.
Your environment
it scans
fully. Programmable?
Artificial intelligence
is forming
this smart robot.

Laura Shovanis a Pushcart Prize nominated poet and a middle grade novelist. Among her award-winning children's books are *The Last Fifth Grade of Emerson Elementary, Takedown,* and *A Place at the Table,* written with Saadia Faruqi. Laura is a longtime poet-in-the-schools. She teaches at Vermont College of Fine Arts.

MessageChatGPT // Linda Mitchell

Tell me how
I can get good grades–straight As, please
and make varsity
bank enough for
     class ring, prom, international field trip
keep my phone off *1st bell to last bell*
get rid of my zits and stinky armpits
do enough chores to keep parents happy
remain the apple of my grandparent's eyes
practice my instrument
turn-in my homework
complete community service
write this admissions essay
     all about me when
     I don't know which parts of myself
     are real and what parts would make
     my first choice school happy
get to bed for plenty of sleep
and wake up in time for first period
hang with my friends
     but stay off the screen
know what to say when asked,
     What do you want to be?
keep my heart from thumping through my shirt
     when BAE walks in
Read.
Tell me, ChatGPT, how, where
     can I find time, find some peace?

Linda Mitchell is a family girl, school librarian and creative person. She hangs out with her laptop, scissors, glue and paper from discarded books to make crafts with two mischievous young cats. Her favorite game is cribbage. She has published in several journals and weekly to her Poetry Friday blog, *A Word Edgewise*.

Things Just Don't Work Like They Used To // Darius Phelps

I used to be someone of great...
Strength.
Caliber.
Respect.
Wisdom.

Nowadays, I am looked down on
instead of looked up to..

Their frowning faces, mocking tones
leave my mind, body, & soul
feeling
oh so *cold*

I miss the warmth
of their genuine smiles
& the eyes of the child
who couldn't wait for me
to share my knowledge
my craft.
my power!

Now, in a world full of technology
one I can't control & *don't understand*
I've become what I have always feared....
being viewed as useless, desolate, and even obsolete.

For this has been no mere game of trick or treat
maybe it's time... I finally admit...defeat
My passion has become...
extinct.

things just don't work
like they used to

Darius Phelps is a PhD candidate at Teachers College, Columbia University. An educator, poet, spoken word artist, and activist, Darius writes poems about grief, liberation, emancipation, and reflection through the lens of a teacher of color, as well as experiencing Black boy joy.

Just essays

love land world futures being

A Vision for Inclusive Campuses: Balancing Comfort and Conflict Through Dialogue //Alana Mondschein

Last summer I attended the Hillel International Global Student Assembly over Shabbat. This created the challenge of having a Shabbat morning service that was comfortable for all students, whether they preferred mixed or separate seating. The solution was a tri-chitza, a mechitza (a divider) that had three sections: men, women, and mixed. I was sitting with a member of the Hillel student cabinet at lunch and everyone was complaining: I hated it–why was there mixed seating; I hated it –why was there separated seating. Then, she remarked that's the joy of the tri-cheitza, no one is happy but everyone is comfortable. We all were complaining but the full mens, womens, and mixed sections showed no one felt so uncomfortable that they could not pray that morning or left to form a prayer group of their own elsewhere.

I think we can learn a lot from the tri-chitza. Both the pro-Israel and anti-Israel students are always going to think the university should be doing something else, preferably that groups idea of what is correct. Yet, how can we at the same time ensure everyone is comfortable on campus, even if they are not happy with some actions. Pushing all students to sit in tense conversations and to hear those they disagree with while at the same time ensuring everyone is comfortable on campus. To me that is when a valuable education and experience for a diverse group of students will take place: no one is happy but everyone will be comfortable.

Right now we are not at a point where Jewish students feel comfortable on campus. I want to make it clear that I am not scared to be Jewish. I am frustrated by a lack of dialogue and exhausted from constantly having to defend my Judaism and Zionism. Nonetheless, I am proud of my identity. I wear my Hebrew name necklace and an Israeli flag pin on my backpack every day with pride. However, antisemitism on campus is not just uncomfortable background noise but it actively makes it difficult for students like me to engage in our studies.

At the beginning of my college career I ran for freshmen representative of the Jewish Student Association. I got the position and directly before my first meeting with the JSA I encountered my first experience with antisemitism on GW's campus. I got to the second floor of the Hillel building a few hours early to write an essay, blissfully unaware that there was a GW for Israel event happening on the roof. As I typed away I began to hear chanting outside the building. Students with Palestinian flags had gathered outside of the building to protest the speaker GWI was hosting. I informed a Hillel staff member of what was going on and she instructed me to stay in the building until she got further information. I was on the second floor alone for an hour while protestors yelled at me, the only person they could see in the building due to everyone else being on the roof. According to the protestors yelling at me I was a war criminal and had the blood of Palestinians on my hands. It was only because I had chosen to be in a Jewish space that these accusations were thrown at me, they knew nothing of my actual beliefs on the conflict.

Flash forward to this year, a few weeks after October 7th. Now the Jewish Student Association Co-President I was responsible for helping set up Shabbat dinner. I showed up to begin my normal routine of laying out table clothes and pouring grape juice. However, as I crossed H street I realized I could see directly into the first floor, not something I had been able to do for a while because we had put up posters of the hostages in the large Hillel windows to advocate for them to be brought home. The rest of my Shabbat evening was spent talking on the phone with Hillel staff, helping tap people into the building because due to security concerns we could not leave the doors unlocked for services and dinner, and filing a police report. Our holy, peaceful Shabbat felt completely violated due to someone else's decision to tear down our posters in our building beforehand.

Despite rising tensions on campus, I am proud of what the Jewish community has accomplished and our refusal to abandon hope.

As the Israel Policy Forum Atid Fellow on campus I hosted three learning cohorts over the last year. Speakers included experts on Israeli policy, experts on Palestinian affairs, including a Palestinian activist, and an expert on Middle East peace building. It gave Jewish students a space to question and explore their beliefs about Israel. There were tense moments, for sure. Hillel's Israel Fellow and the Palestinian activist had a long debate over the word occupation and the tension was palpable. However, everyone came away from these conversations with a better understanding of their own beliefs and others beliefs. And, at the end of that tense conversation the Israeli and Palestinian voices got up and shook hands. Yes, many people were unhappy with views shared in the learning cohort and many students disagreed greatly with each other. But, everyone was comfortable enough to come back to the table for the next meeting.

I can guarantee you we can find a way to make all students comfortable on campus even if, like the tri-chitza, students are still unhappy with certain decisions. There might be a lot of complaining, but it will be accompanied by an expanded understanding of one another, greater empathy, and less hatred. Antisemitism must be addressed on campus but in a way that does not just combat one act of antisemitism, rather one that works to promote greater understanding so that Jewish students can feel comfortable on campus and the hard conversations can begin.

Alana Mondschein (she/her/hers) is a third year student at the George Washington University Elliott School of International Affairs studying Middle Eastern Studies. She was the 2023-2024 Jewish Student Association Co-President and Israel Policy Forum Atid Fellow. Alana delivered the above speech at the GW Summer Institute on Antisemitism.

Compulsory Service // S.

It was the start of my first high school year when I met my forever love. I liked him immediately, and in August 2020 we started dating. Everything was perfect. I still can't believe it was real. But on September 27 war began.

> Large-scale fighting began on the morning of 27 September. For more than 30 years Artsahk has been the center of a conflict between Armenia and Azerbaijan. Both countries claim the territory and have dug their armies in along its borders. These explosions were the start of another round of fighting.

It is hard to describe what we felt during that time. Boys who studied with us were dying, being killed and tortured.

The decision was made. He should leave Armenia just to stay alive.

I love my homeland, but I love him more than anything. I will never forget the eyes that were always the bravest, filled with tears saying our good-byes, knowing it may be forever.

Today is the 12th of July 2024. It's been more than three years we haven't seen each other. I miss him endlessly. I miss his physical presence with me. These years never separated us; they just made us stronger.

Two days ago, I visited Yerablur; on a hilltop overlooking the capital city of Yerevan, our soldiers are buried there. Most of them were born in 2000-2002. I am glad he was not there with me. Each grave has a photograph of a fallen soldier. Any could be him. I recalled, looking into the eyes of our friend memorialized, that I had stupidly, without thinking, expressed to my love that I was happy he was not in Armenia. He felt very guilty.

I do everything for my homeland to blossom and become better, but I am not ready to give him away.

I hug my pillow every night and morning crying and missing. I really wish it was you. The distance is killing me. I wish one day you will hug me again.

S. is a college student and English teacher in Armenia.

Just
fiction

love land world futures being

My Jam Jar Ghost // Shih-Li Kow

I caught a ghost the other day. There were many ghosts in Mrs. Tan's house, but this was the first one I'd caught. It happened when I was reading aloud a story about a girl and a dragon to Mrs. Tan. I thought she was asleep, but she asked me to repeat the name of the girl. *Ai Ping,* I said. I looked at her and wondered if it was her who'd spoken or one of the ghosts because I'd replaced the girl's name with mine when I was reading.

Mrs. Tan's son paid me to read to her for an hour every evening. He lived down the street, but he said he couldn't stay with her himself. He said it was complicated and I wouldn't understand. So, I didn't ask why and went every day after school. Sometimes, I stayed for an extra hour or I'd put the radio on until the national anthem played at midnight. Sitting with a dying woman who never talked back was peaceful, and the ghosts never did anything more than tug at my hair on occasion. It was better than all the screaming and yelling that went on in my own house. Sometimes, I stayed the whole night. If Mrs. Tan's son saw me leave in the mornings, he never asked me why either.

The ghost I caught had floated across the room quite nonchalantly. It hung in the air — sometimes opaque, sometimes gauzy. I snagged it just as it turned white against the dark green curtains of Mrs. Tan's room. I pinched its tail and coiled it around my index finger.

It didn't look like much, this long white worm of a ghost. It didn't feel like much either. It had no weight, only a sort of damp coldness which tugged my finger like a string on a helium balloon. It was hard to believe I'd caught a ghost so easily. Collectors used all types of traps and special lights, but there were so many ghosts in Mrs. Tan's house that I suppose I shouldn't have been surprised to pluck a small one out of the air just like that.

I pressed my thumb against it to keep it from unraveling while I rummaged for something to contain it. I found a glass jar in the kitchen that looked like it would do the job. When I woke up in the morning, the ghost had wriggled into the spaces between the threads in the lid and was already half out of the jar. I pushed it back in and tightened the lid. I put the jar in a fishbowl filled with water and weighed it down with a can of sardines. I told Mrs. Tan I'd caught her a dragon and I thought I saw her smile.

My ghost didn't seem to have friends. I kept it on Mrs. Tan's bedside table when I was reading to her, but no other ghost came looking for it. And there were many others, big and small ones that were all over the house: in the backs of cupboards and ceiling corners, under the beds, in the trees out in the garden, under the sink in the bathroom, behind every door, and even amongst the pots in the kitchen. I guessed the ghost I had must've been a bit of an outcast.

It stopped trying to escape after I put it in the fishbowl and stayed curled up at the bottom of its jam jar. If I tapped the jar, it would perk up a little. I wondered if ghosts could die if they were already dead. I wondered which made them sadder, wandering around all alone and being ignored or the attentions of a captor and a glass jar prison.

I attempted to sell it. There were people who collected these things, although mine was hardly an impressive specimen. I put up a post on eBay: *Small ghost for sale. Low maintenance.* There were two inquiries. They wanted photographs, but I didn't have the equipment to take a photograph of a ghost. It didn't show up when I used the camera on my phone. They wanted to know the exact measurements and condition of the ghost. I replied: *Approximately eight inches long. Condition is fair.* They asked for its pedigree and origin. I stopped replying. Anyway, I was getting fond of it, my first ghost.

I thought of releasing it in a place where it had friends or where there were ghosts of the same kind, but I didn't know where worm-like ghosts hung out. The black, pumpkin-faced ones liked to play under Mrs. Tan's bed and the banshees usually lounged in the trees, but I didn't know about the plain, quiet ones like the one I had. It seemed to me that my ghost might get bullied by the alpha ghosts. So, I kept it in the jar while I tried to figure out what to do.

One night, not long after I had caught the ghost, Mrs. Tan took a turn for the worse. Her every breath sounded like a drowning gasp. I called her son, the man who paid me to watch her. He came quickly and held her hand, his head bowed low. He did not see the ghost that came out of her mouth with her last breath, a white wisp approximately eight inches long.

I opened the jam jar and let my ghost out. It squirmed a little this way and that, straightening its kinks after being stuck in the jar for so long. The two of them, my ghost and Mrs. Tan's, floated towards the door together like a pair of jellyfish tentacles. A pair of dragon worms. I could've reached out and caught them both. I could've given them to Mrs. Tan's son in a jar, but it felt right just to let them be. The same way it felt right just to let the man cry.

Shih-Li Kow is the author of *Ripples and Other Stories* and *Bone Weight and Other Stories*. The French edition (translated by Frederic Grellier) of her novel, *The Sum of Our Follies*, won the 2018 Prix du Premier Roman Etranger. She lives in Kuala Lumpur, Malaysia. www.shihlikow.com

Just teaching

love   land   world   futures   being

poetry · flash fiction · essays

How to Use This Book

This anthology is a gift of young adult literature, crafted to center and amplify youth experiences. It is designed to be a versatile tool in the hands of educators who understand the power of literature to engage, inspire, and educate. While we trust that teachers, as experienced educators, have the pedagogical knowledge and creativity to seamlessly integrate these texts into your existing curriculum, this chapter aims to provide additional ideas and insights to enhance your teaching practice with details that we hope also support new-to-the-profession educators. Our goal is to offer a range of strategies and lesson plans that support literary comprehension, critical reading, and the enjoyment of literature in your classroom.

Embracing the Joy of Reading

At its core, this anthology is meant to be enjoyed. The poems, short stories, and essays are selected not only for their literary merit but also for their ability to resonate with young readers. Encouraging students to find pleasure in reading is a foundational goal, and we hope this collection sparks a love for literature that transcends the classroom. As you explore the texts with your students, consider creating an environment that celebrates reading as a joyful and enriching activity. Allow students to immerse themselves in the narratives, relate to the characters, and find their own connections to the themes presented. You may want to start with reading the "Choice Literature" section or "Four Quarters of Choice Reading."

Strategy Lessons for Literary Comprehension

While enjoyment is paramount, we also recognize the importance of guiding students toward deeper literary comprehension and critical analysis. In this chapter, we present several strategy lessons that you may find familiar but are worth revisiting with a fresh perspective. Each lesson is designed to align with the key themes of the anthology, providing structured approaches to exploring the texts. From "pair shares" that facilitate collaborative learning to characterization activities like the Place Poem, these lessons offer concrete methods for delving into the literary elements and themes of the anthology. There is also a lesson inspired from the National Writing Project around tone that can be adapted for many English language arts topics.

Centering Youth Experiences

The texts in this anthology are carefully curated to reflect and center youth experiences. This focus not only makes the literature more relatable and engaging for students but also provides a platform for discussing broader social and emotional issues. Lessons such as "Justice Literature Circles" and "Reading Poetry Relationally" encourage students to connect personally and emotionally with the texts, fostering a deeper understanding and empathy. These activities help students see themselves and their peers in the literature, making the reading experience more meaningful and impactful.

Fostering Choice and Voice

Empowering students with choice is a powerful motivator in the classroom. This anthology supports choice reading, allowing students to select texts that interest them and speak to their personal experiences. The chapter includes strategies for integrating choice reading into your curriculum, such as "Choice Reading with Reading Conferences" and the "Four Quarters of Choice Reading: A Progression." These methods not only promote student autonomy but also provide opportunities for individualized instruction and meaningful reading experiences.

Innovative Approaches to Reading Response

In addition to traditional reading and discussion activities, this chapter explores innovative approaches to reading response. For example, "Vlogging as Embodied Reading Response" offers a modern twist on the classic book report, allowing students to use digital media to express their interpretations and connections to the texts. This approach not only caters to diverse learning styles but also embraces the digital literacy skills that are increasingly important in today's world.

Vocabulary and Literary Analysis

Lastly, we address the ever-important aspect of vocabulary instruction and literary analysis. "The Answer to Vocabulary Instruction" provides practical strategies for integrating vocabulary development into your reading activities, ensuring that students not only understand the texts but also expand their linguistic repertoire. Through these methods, students will be better equipped to analyze and appreciate the rich language and nuanced themes present in the anthology.

In conclusion, while this anthology is intended to be a space for students to enjoy and engage with young adult literature, this chapter offers a wealth of ideas and strategies to help you make the most of these texts in your classroom. We hope these lessons inspire you to explore new approaches and deepen your students' love for literature.

Pair Share

This discussion strategy is ubiquitous because it is grounded in relationality – students talking to the person next to them– and offers time and space for students to process what they are learning, which can be extended by surfacing the many ideas of class members.

To Prepare

Copy any text from the anthology. In this example, we focus on a Just Love selection. There is a digital version online, but you can also take a picture of the book and share it with students via the learning management system (Canvas, Google Classroom). If you have printers in your school, you can make a copy for each student to tape into their notebook.

Launch the Lesson

In the National Writing Project style, we suggest beginning each class with a "write into the day.". Give the student a few prompts so they have some choices as to what to write about. If you are reading from Just Love, you might ask them to write from 3 modes:

1. Information: Define love;
2. Argument: Take a stand on the phrase "I love X" and if people are too loose with this word;
3. Narrative: Write a time you fell in love – with a person, a pet, food, etc. Take us into the moment through dialogue and sensory language.

Set the time for 5 minutes and use your writing norms. We like "no walk, no talk" so that everyone protects that writing space. You can have students write in their paper or digital notebook. We like paper notebooks because it is a break from technology. As always follow any accommodations students need.

Reading from *Just YA*

Select a text from the Just Love section so that you can keep the theme going from the write-in. Pass out the story– in paper form or digitally. These texts are short enough to read multiple times, so try a few different ways:

- *Read it silently, independently* and notice what you notice. Invite students to highlight or annotate favorite lines, words that sound good to them, ideas that resonate, questions that emerge. Very broad.

- *Teacher read-aloud.* Before you read it aloud, be sure to read it to yourself and that you know the pronunciation and rhythm. This will make for a fluent reading of the story, and students can enjoy the sound as much as the ideas.
- *Guided reading.* Invite students to make a t-chart in their notebook. Ask students to predict what the text will be about based on the title. Read the first chunk and unpack the key who, what, where, when to monitor student reading. Read on to notice the author's craft (metaphor, simile, line breaks, dialogue) and consider why. Read on to the ending and consider the so what or what the author's commentary on humanity or the genre or the thematic topic might be.

Get Moving: Stand and Talk

Get students' bodies moving by sending partners to various corners of the room to stand and talk about their write-in and the text. Project on the board this question:

> Which mode did you write about today regarding Just Love (or any other theme) and how would the author/narrator of today's text respond to that prompt? Give evidence from the text to support your response.

For fun, you can suggest the partner whose birthday is closest to today's date respond first. The teacher's role during this time is to move around the room listening, maybe taking some notes.

Closure

After 5 or so minutes bring the class together and synthesize what you heard, asking various partners to share out themes and insights around love, and what is "just" or justice oriented about the student write-ins and the author's short text on this subject.

Note: You can repeat this lesson with any of the themes (e.g., being, land, world, futures) and/or specific writing forms (e.g., poem, flash fiction, essay).

Characterization: Place Poem

This comprehension strategy is better known as a get-to-know-you activity and poem from George Ella Lyon that teachers use at the beginning of the school year because it is a really accessible list poem. We want to know our students and for our students to know one another. We also want our students to know the authors they are reading are human beings, too. The authors in this anthology are living authors with lives within and beyond these stories.

To Prepare

Copy any short fiction from the anthology. There is a digital version online, but you can also take a picture of the book and share it with students via the learning management system (Canvas, Google Classroom). If you have printers in your school, you can make a copy for each student to tape into their notebook.

Launch the Lesson

Start with a write-in. Project three options on the white-board or overhead project for students to select from (or make these available on your learning management system). A note about these write-ins, students should feel free to reject the prompts or develop their own during the writing time. For this prompt focused on place and where we are from, here are a few suggestions:

1. Informational: Write 5 facts about where you are from. It can be where you live now or where you lived once. Imagine your writing as a travel brochure and these are places to go in your town.

2. Argument: The places we live shape who we become. Agree or disagree. First, tell us where you life or places you have lived. Then, consider both sides: *On one hand, I agree… On the other hand, I could disagree…. However, if I had to choose, I'd say.*

3. Narrative: Tell a story about a place that makes you most feel safe and or happy. Your happy place. When do you go there? Who is there? What makes you feel safe or happy?

Reading from *Just YA*

Distribute the text or direct students to locate the text within the anthology. This lesson works especially well if you select several stories so that more perspectives are included in the conversation around characters' sense of place.

The short fiction seems to work best for this so that you can examine character traits and support a connection between where the student-reader is from and the character-narrator is from in the text. Here are the steps:

- **Step 1**: Read the short fiction independently, as a teacher read aloud, or as guided reading.
- **Step 2**: Step into the shoes of the character. Make a list of any character's attributes. List details about the story: setting, conflicts, important plot points, themes, etc.
- **Step 3**: Using the template, create a "Where I Am From" poem about your favorite character.
- **Step 4**: Think of opposing figures in the story novel (antagonist and protagonist) and juxtapose these two characters to create a poem for two voices.

Get Moving: Open Mic

After students have written their poems, have a poetry open mic. Allow students to share their poems and peers to guess the characters revealed in the poems. Or use the open mic as a replacement for book talks/reports.

Closure

In a discussion or pair-share reflection, return to the write-in prompts to talk about the argument question: *In what ways does place shape us, and in what ways do we shape place?* What is our responsibility in the places we share with others if this is true?

Tone of Just Being

Tone is a tough concept to teach, sometimes because it is taught with mood but more often because the texts are not written for youth or made to connect to lives of youth. When we ask about the tone of the piece, we are asking readers to decipher how the writer feels about or positions themselves within a specific and/or general experience.

To Prepare

This lesson focuses on Just Being, but you can choose any theme. Copy three or more texts from each of the forms – poetry, fiction, and essay. Sharing a variety of forms is key. There is a digital version online, but you can also scan pages of the book and share it with students via the learning management system (Canvas, Google Classroom). If you have printers in your school, you can make a copy for each student to tape into their notebook.

Launch the Lesson

Start with a write-in. Project three options on the white-board or overhead project for students to select from (or make these available on your learning management system). A note about these write-ins, students should feel free to reject the prompts or develop their own during the writing time. For this prompt focused on place and where we are from, here are a few suggestions:

1. Informational: Create a pie chart of how you spend your day or week. Create categories (e.g., sleep, school, work, video games, social media, etc.). Add a legend or label each section. If there is time, write about each slice of the pie.
2. Argument: I am most my Self when I am X (name a place or activity). First, define Self: *On one hand, I am most myself when … On the other hand, I am also myself when…. However, if I had to choose, I'd say…*
3. Narrative: Get ready with me. Take us into the way you "get ready" in the morning or for some activity that you do (e.g., preparing for a video game session, pre-game sport ritual, setting up a place to read or do homework).

Reading from *Just YA*

Distribute the selected texts or direct students to the Just Being section of the anthology. Independently or in pairs, give students some time to read one or two of the pieces. In partners or small groups ask students to talk about this: What is the author trying to say about "being"? Ask a few students to then share out whole class.

Next, students will explore the idea of "tone," in their writing. One way to define tone is as the "attitude the author has toward their subject." Provide students with some tone words. You may want to give them a list of "tone words" like this one, or a shorter modified list (accepting, amused, angry, anxious, bitter, confident, enthusiastic, fond, happy, guilty, indifferent, ironic, joyful, loving, melancholy, nostalgic, proud, poignant, reflective, silly, touchy, upset, vexed, serious, silly).

You may select a poem and read it together first, modeling this process as a think aloud first. In the modeling, focus on this move: What makes you say so? This move is a way of generating text support but also interpretation. Model and invite answers to these questions "How does this author feel about X?' and "how do you know?"

Get Moving: Tonal Gallery Walk

Now, ask students to return to their selected text. Ideally, you would have physical copies of this and can tape them to the wall, but having a digital copy at desks is fine. Give students four sticky notes.

Ask students to provide a one word answer to the question: How does the author feel about the topic in their text? They can put that one sticky note on the back of the text or paper, or set it aside in a notebook so it is not visible to others.

Next, be sure students have three more sticky notes. Tell students to get up and moving to their peers' selected texts. They should find three other texts that their peers selected. Moving around the room, they should read the text and then add a sticky note answering this question: How does this writer feel about their topic? How do you know? Repeat this two more times.

Now students should return to their original selected text and look at the four sticky notes. They should reflect on this range of words, perhaps go to a thesaurus to consider the nuance of these words and consider which seem closest to the author's attitude toward their topic. What accounts for the different readings of tone? Why does it matter that we consider the author's tone as we read?

Why does it matter for us as writers to consider how readers interpret our writing?

Closure

Finally, encourage students to return to their write-in and name the tone of their own writing. Consider, in a pair-share, repeating this sticky note exercise with student writing and give students time to revise their writing if the peer's tone words conflict with the student-writer's intentions. Give them time to revise their papers based on the feedback they received. Are there words or lines they want to take out, change, or add in order to convey the tone they want to?

Note: This strategy was adapted from The National Writing Project's lesson on tone in Coach.Teach.Write.

Justice Literature Circles

Literature Circles engage students in elements of literature (plot sequence, character, setting, conflict, theme, etc.). The preparation for and participating in the discussions support students in making choices about what about the elements matter and how to select text evidence that illuminates the author's craft and purpose. During discussions, students re-read, reflect, retell, and relate to what they read. The group work deepens understanding because readers can check and adjust their meaning-making through dialoguing with peers. Further, the role of personal response on interpretation becomes visible with other readers showing literature as dynamic rather than a static text to be decoded.

The roles offered at the end of this section are a starting point for equitable discussions as each student has a specific contribution to make (e.g., as sequencer or discussion director) with dedicated time to facilitate a discussion around a literary element around what was interesting to them. The roles can be modified and abandoned as students practice these more structured literary discussions or opt for more casual book group routines.

To Prepare

This lesson focuses on fiction because the various literature circle jobs work best with a narrative arc or plot. Make multiple copies of five to seven texts. Class sizes range from 5 to 40 across the country for various reasons. We have found groups of 4 seem to work best, so you will need as many different stories as groups. Of course, we value student choice, so you may invite students to select a story from the anthology they'd like to read and discuss together.

There is a digital version online, but you can also scan pages of the book and share it with students via the learning management system (Canvas, Google Classroom). If you have printers in your school, you can make a copy for each student to tape into their notebook.

For the literature circle jobs, there are six: sequencer, read aloud master, word watcher, discussion director, illustrator, and advice columnist. You can make copies of the instructions (see the end of this section) or post them on your learning management system (LMS). The descriptions include fairly detailed instructions and sentence stems. Please modify these for your students or search the web for other variations.

If you have facilitated this lesson in the past, post examples of the completed jobs (with different stories) on the classroom wall so that students can see mentor texts or examples.

Launch the Lesson

Start with a write-in. Project three options on the white-board or overhead project for students to select from (or make these available on your learning management system). A note about these write-ins, students should feel free to reject the prompts or develop their own during the writing time. For this prompt focused on place and where we are from, here are a few suggestions:

1. Informational: Just. Justice. What do these words mean? Create dictionary entries for these two words with the part of speech, sample sentences, synonyms, and antonyms.
2. Argument: X situation in my life is unjust. (Name a situation). First, define unjust, then explain the situation. Then, consider perspectives: *On one hand, some would say X is unjust because... On the other hand, some would say X is unjust because.... However, if I had to choose, I'd say...*
3. Narrative: Tell the story of a time when you felt or witnessed something unjust happening. Take us into the scene with dialogue or use sensory language to describe the setting (smell, taste, touch, colors, textures, temperature, etc.). Get right into the unjust moment because this is a quick write.

Reading from *Just YA*

There are several ways you can set up the reading groups

1. Students can preview the stories and then rank which ones they want to read. You can group by interests. Then, students can negotiate which roles they want to do. There are six options, so not all the roles will be used each time
2. Students can make their own groups and then negotiate among members which text they are going to read along with which role they will step into. It is important for students to know their role before they read so that they are reading with a particular lens (character, setting, language, conflict).
3. You can make the groups and assign texts based on class dynamics or what you know about your students. If you've

made most of the decisions, it might be nice to let students decide or negotiate which literary role they will take up.

4. Note: Because the stories are short, you can do all of the above. Students can switch groups and stories over the course of several days or weeks. You may even make a certain day of the week Literature Circle Day.

Distribute the literature circle role instructions. Students benefit from knowing their role before they start reading so that they know what to attend to or have a reading purpose. Distribute the texts in print. A hardcopy is helpful for students to annotate (e.g., underline or circle parts they want to focus on for their role). Also, when it comes time for discussion, having the roles and texts in hard copy keep students focused on the discussion together and off technology.

Give students a class period to read independently and work on their role. Your role during this is to confer with each reader and support their process. As you confer, ask questions about "just" and "justice" and "unjust" so that you can support students in uncovering common themes across the texts. Ask follow-up questions as you meet with students such as "what makes you say so" to encourage this kind of discussion when they meet with their groups. We want students to cite text evidence and ask follow-up questions for rich discussion.

Get Moving: Discussion Time

The next day, unless you have block scheduling, you will want to set up a protocol for discussion. I like to divide the class time by the number of group members so that each member has a dedicated time to facilitate. For example if you have a 50-minute class period and four group members, the protocol may look like this:

- 5 minutes of setting up the room or gathering in groups spread out across the room or in the school library
- 10 minutes per group member
- 5 minutes for reflection or assessment
- Your role is to set a timer on the board to help students with pacing and to walk around and support the discussion. You may want to offer students a handout (or co-create a document) about group norms with sentences stems:
- I'll get things started with the first question. Everyone turn to page (#) as I read.

186

- Thank you (name), for your question. Here's what I think.
- I hear so and so saying (this), and I'd like to suggest (this).
- Does anyone else want add on to that?
- (name), will you ask the next question, please.
- On page ___, the character says ____, so this shows _____.
- I didn't notice that when I read first read it, but thanks (name).
- What makes you say so?

Closure

Return to the write-ins from the day before. And ask students to talk about the role of justice in their readings and conversations. Encourage the groups to reflect on their discussion skills: What went well? What could be improved? What kinds of questions or roles were most helpful in deepening an understanding of justice? Did the roles create greater equity in the conversation so that no one had to carry the load? Or did the roles feel restrictive? What would you like to change for next time?

As the teacher, you might share some of your observations. Provide feedback on their roles and contributions. Highlight strengths and areas for improvement. In subsequent sessions, rotate the roles within each group so that all students experience different responsibilities. Repeat the literature circle process, adjusting texts and groups as necessary based on student progress and interest.

Literature Circle Roles and Descriptions

sequencer, read aloud master, word watcher, discussion director, illustrator, and advice columnist.

Sequencer

Write eight sentences that include the important events that occurred during the reading of just the chunk that was assigned. Each sentence should be a different event. For each event, be sure you have included the answers to the following questions: Who? Did What? When? and Where? **Cut out** the sentences so that each one is on a separate slip of paper.

When your group meets, have them put the events in order. Staple the slips of paper in this order. Decide together which sentence tells the most important thing that happened in your reading, and place a **star** next to it and discuss why. Turn this in!

Read-aloud Master

Select <u>three</u> passages from the text from different parts of the text that are important or interesting throughout the chunk. Mark these passages with a sticky note and write the page/paragraph on a separate sheet of paper. After you choose your passages, you must explain the author's purpose for each passage using the format below.. In other words, what message was the author trying to get across or why was that part included?

When your group meets, you may read the passages aloud to the group, or ask another person to read the selection. After your group reads each one, discuss why the author included that part in the story. Allow your group members to share their thoughts first. Then share what you wrote in the sheet/notebook entry you wrote in the format below.

You will turn in a typed paper with the page numbers, a brief paraphrase of the paragraphs, explanation of the author's purpose for each passage, and notes from the discussion. It should look like this:

Passage 1:

      Page number:

      What's basically happening in this passage?

      Why is this worth bringing to the circle for discussion?

      Notes from the group discussion:

Passage 2:

Page number:
What's basically happening in this passage?
Why is this worth bringing to the circle for discussion?
Notes from the group discussion:
Passage 3:
Page number:
What's basically happening in this passage?
Why is this worth bringing to the circle for discussion?
Notes from the group discussion:

Word Watcher

Your job is to find and define vocabulary words from the day's reading in DIFFERENT SECTIONS of the text. As you read, choose words that you think are interesting, confusing, or new to you. Or choose the most important word in a few chapters through the text. Write each word, the page number where the word is found, the sentence in which the word is used, and the dictionary definition of the word on a separate sheet of paper (typed). Be ready to tell your group why you chose these words.

This is how your paper should look:
1. Word _____ Page # _____
 Sentence from reading
 Dictionary definition:
 Connotation as used in the sentence:

2. Word _____ Page # _____
 Sentence from reading
 Dictionary definition:
 Connotation as used in the sentence:

3. Word _____ Page # _____
 Sentence from reading
 Dictionary definition:
 Connotation as used in the sentence:

4. Word _____ Page # _____
 Sentence from reading
 Dictionary definition:
 Connotation as used in the sentence:

5. Word _____Page # _____
Sentence from reading
Dictionary definition:
Connotation as used in the sentence:

Discussion Director

Create 4 thoughtful questions for your group to answer orally. You must create two discussion questions from each of the four categories: literal, inferential, interpretive and your own thoughts. Print these on paper with space to take notes on the group's responses and ideas on the day of the literature circle.

Literal Questions (Right There Questions - the answer is right there in the story. You can point to the answer. The words used to make up the question are often the same words that are in the answer):

- On page ___, what happens is _____Define the meaning of
- On page ___, what happens is _____Where was Name as many
- On page ___, what happens is _____Describe in your own words
- On page ___, what happens is _____What happened when
- On page ___, what happens is _____What are the characters doing to solve the problem of
- Which character
- On page ___, what happens is _____
- OR create your own literal questions.

Inferential Questions (Think and Search Questions - the answer is in the text, but it needs to be put together with different pieces of information from the book. You have to think and search for the answer):

- How would you compare
- Choose the best
- How could the character
- What is the difference between
- OR create your own inferential questions.

Interpretive Questions (the Author and Me Questions - you need to think about what you know and what the author has said in the text. The answer will be from both the author and you as you infer meaning. The answer won't be found on the printed page, but the information to answer the question is there):

- On page ___, what happens is _____Predict what would happen if _____
- On page ___, what's going on is _____Why did the author include _____
- On page ____, what is confusing is that _____Can you prove that _____
- On page _____, what happens is _____What was the author's purpose when _____
- On page_____, what is going on is _____Why did the character _____
- OR create your own interpretive questions.

<u>My Own Thoughts</u>. The answer is not in the story. The question is asking for your own thoughts about something in the story. It can be creative or open-ended and there is no right or wrong answer, but the answer should be supported by the text and your personal experiences and beliefs.

- On page ___, what happens is _____Assess how you would feel if _____
- On page ___, what happens is _____How would you improve _____
- On page ___, what happens is _____How did you feel when _____
- On page ___, what happens is _____Why do you think _____
- On page ___, what happens is _____Was it fair when _____
- OR create your own "my thoughts" questions.

Illustrator

On a sheet of paper, draw a picture of something that is connected specifically to your book. It can be displayed as a cartoon, chart, diagram, or a sketch. Some examples are a character, the setting, a problem, an exciting part, a surprise or a prediction. Document the page number and passage that inspired you.

When your group meets, do not tell what the drawing is. Let them guess and talk about it first and observe them. Then you can tell about it. Have your group title the picture. With your group, write a brief description telling the significance of the picture on the reverse side of the illustration. Your description should explain something that can't be seen by looking at the picture. Do not just describe the picture. Turn this in!

Advice Columnist

What is the conflict in the story? Choose a character from your story who is affected by the problem or conflict. Pretend you are that character and write a letter to "Dear Hank and John" explaining your problem. John and Hank Green (authors and YouTubers) offer both humorous and heartfelt advice about life's big and small questions on their podcast. .Be sure to give accurate background knowledge of the situation for the brothers and a complete description of the conflict – try to sound like the character paying attention to any common phrases and tone. Don't forget to sign your letter as the character! (Research "friendly letters" and who Hank and John are – or sub them out for another advice podcaster or YouTuber.)

When your group meets, share the letter by reading it aloud. On the back of the letter (or another place), your group should write a "Dear Hank and John" letter back to your character sounding like an adviser or counselor. Include ideas on how the character can solve the conflict. Turn this in!

Reading Poetry Relationally

In this lesson, I, Sarah, take you into my junior high classroom to offer you a glimpse into a lesson in progress. I invite you to step into a poetry lesson that creates space for collaborative interpretation and some quiet opportunities for students to do some concentrated and repeated readings. This is great when you need a low-key day in the classroom to assuage anxiety or off-set some tense energy going on in the school.

———————

"Find a good place to stop in your books," I said to end our choice-reading time.

I finished up a student-reading conference and looked around to see students finishing a page, writing a response on a sticky note, stretching their legs.

"Today we're going to spend a little bit of time thinking about poetry around the topics of justice and being a young adult. Some of our time has been on novel study or textbook readings, so I thought we'd spend some time with poetry," I said.

"Yes," one student whispered to a neighbor.

"No," one another whispered to a neighbor.

"Right, so mixed responses — to the poetry? I think poetry has typically been written for little kids or adults. A lot of the poems in textbooks seem to be about historical periods or written long ago. I want us to take a look at poems written by contemporary poets.

"You have likely learned poetry in different ways in elementary school — a unit of study, some writing of poetry. Poems are not actually written for students to analyze. Poems are a very concentrated form of ideas and experiences — big, complex ideas condensed, concentrated into phrases. Powerful words and images about those ideas seem mysterious to readers because phrases and fragments want the reader to think about what's there and what's not. What I like about poetry –its form — is that it accepts that sometimes ideas and stories and experiences are partial or incomplete.

"Now what does this have to do justice and being a young adult? The concentrated and fragmented form helps people process the fragments of understanding that they can piece together in snapshots - stories, thoughts, observations, even arguments," I said.

The room was quiet, so I thought the mood was right to begin. I appreciated their patience and respect. I continued

"Let's read a few poems to consider what these poets have to say about and to us, young adults. Open you Chromebooks. " I paused.

Students open up their Chromebooks, log into our Google classroom, and open up the shared document of poems we can all edit. I copy and pasted a bunch of poems from *Just YA* into one Google doc for collaborative reading and commenting. I made copies of this document for each class period.

The reason for the collaborative document is that I wanted us to all be inside this document of poems together, trying to make sense of poems in a shared, live experience without me pacing their reading or controlling their focus.

I asked students to first scan the titles and forms to get a sense of the whole and notice that all the poems are short. They realized quickly that they would have time to read multiple poems, but this scanning helps them get excited about what is interesting to them.

I asked students to use the comment feature to just comment openly about what they like, what they notice, what they are wondering. I reminded students that they were connected to the World Wide Web and that they can, at any point, look up the poet. Search up a word. Explore a place.

For students who wanted some guidance, I offered these questions on a half-sheet of paper (handout):

1. What do you know about the speaker? His/her relationship to the audience, concerns, purpose for saying these words?
2. What is the setting or sense of place in this poem? Which words/phrases are most vivid or create an image/picture?
3. Which words capture the mood throughout the poem?
4. Which words seem fancy or unfamiliar? Find the denotation or dictionary definition of a few words.
5. Which lines or phrases teach us about 9/11? What does the poet want us to know or remember?
6. Describe the form of the poem: how many lines; does it rhyme; how many syllables in each line, most common punctuation.
7. Notice any figurative language: simile, metaphor, allusion, personification, alliteration, onomatopoeia, hyperbole.

Students read, selected phrases, and attached comments to the phrases. I noticed some students opening up a new tab to look up a word, an allusion, an image. They were uncovering meaning, reading into the white spaces the poet left open.

I kept the lights low and turned on some lo-fi background music. Other than that, the classroom was silent.

I hovered in different spots of the room making myself available for quiet conversations about the poems. One boy calls me over with a wave.

"This poem here doesn't have a meter and doesn't rhyme. I don't think I have anything to comment on," one student says in a whisper. "Should I do something else?"

I kneel down and take a look at the poem he's referring to.

"I see what you mean. This is a free verse poem. There isn't a pattern. It doesn't rhyme. We are both noticing the same thing. But let's think about why that is. A poet crafts each line-break purposefully, so if the form doesn't follow a regular pattern, that might be for a reason. If we think about the subject of land and how the poet must have been feeling, it makes sense that there's lots of irregularity or uncertainty. It's possible that the poet is trying to capture the chaos with this irregular meter," I whispered.

The boy had an "aha" look in his eyes and returns the poem.

"I'm a little confused. Can you help me?" another student asked in a whisper-shout waving me over. She is reading "A Place to Breathe" by Christine Hartman Derr. "The speaker in this poem seems to be Native American? I don't know what some of these words mean. "

"Aha, I see what you mean. Let's read this together. the author wrote 'Wado, ganolvvsgv,/gratitude for wind, for breezes.' And just above that there is 'a language maybe I used to know'. Yes, it seems this poet is exploring language – the knowing, the forgotten words. Maybe something about connections. What else are you noticing here?"

Students had an opportunity to make some comments on their selected poem and noticed peers commenting, too, so I interrupted the quiet to move into the online discussion part. Time for students to respond to each other's noticings online.

"Okay, so finish up the comment you're making right now. And then go to the top of the poem and read the observations and comments your poem-mates noted. If you click on the comment, you'll see that you can reply to one another. See if this helps you notice new features of your poem, if this extends your understanding of the poems, justice, and being a young adult."

Before we ended class, I ask students to return to Google classroom and write a public comment on the assignment: "One poem I read was "_____," and one thing I learned/found interesting, powerful, insightful, meaningful is _____ because _____."

In closing, I thanked students for their silent dialogue, compassion, and thoughtful work as we closed class. One boy told me he opened his notebook during the activity to write a poem inspired by Stefani Boutelier's "Zit Ode." I listen and then invite others to try a poem. They can access the Google doc and the anthology online any time they wish. I tell them that I'd love to read their poetry.

You don't have to do a poetry unit for students to read a poem. You don't have to do a lot of frontloading of poetry analysis methods or figurative language for students to be able to access the meaning of a poem. Gather a few poems; create a few questions; and then let students uncover the poetry. The poem itself is enough to start the conversation. Students will dialogue about meaning with one another to uncover meaning, illuminate the poet's craft, and respond with their hearts and minds.

As Pablo Neruda said (or I think it was Neruda), "Poetry is an act of peace." And don't we need more peace now? Don't wait until April (National Poetry Month) to welcome poetry into your classes.

Choice Reading with Reading Conferences

Just YA is online, and students can spend the first five to ten minutes of class reading any and all of the poems, stories, and essays. The point is that they are actually reading during class time because the texts are written for them by incredible authors who deeply respect young adult readers (and their teachers).

Now what do you do? How do you support students in their choice reading? How can you use this time to do some instruction or extension work with your students? First, you may not need to do anything, but we have found that conferring is a great way to assess your students interests, strengths, and needs.

You may think: *But everyone is quiet and happy. I don't want to interrupt them.*

You may think: *Should I be reading, too? All that SSR and DEAR says I should be modeling what good readers do, but, hey, if they are reading, then they can't see me modeling, and isn't what's going on in my mind and heart more important than my book-reading posture?*

You may think: *Maybe I will just take this opportunity to send a few parent emails or read those surveys I gave them yesterday.*

While getting administrative work done is tempting, don't do it. Instead, start conversations. When students are reading, it is the golden opportunity for you to do the very important work of teachers that is neglected in so many PDs and teacher ed programs: reading instruction and assessment.

3 Goals of a Reading Conference

First, assess who they are as human beings. This may sound like any of these questions: Tell me about what are you reading. Do you have any experiences with this (whatever is going on in the text)? Why did you choose this text or what would you have chosen to read? What are you doing after school today? Tell me about your "typical" after-school routine.

Next, you can assess their comprehension of the text. Try any of these conversation starters: What's going on? How do you know? Read that paragraph. What seems to be most important in that paragraph? How do you know? Tell me about why the author might have written this book, created that interaction, titled the chapter this way.

Finally, use the conversation to help you plan for instruction. Try any of these prompts: What in your reading is unfamiliar? What do you want to understand better? What is a word or phrase in this that is unfamiliar? What are you noticing about the author's writing style?

All of this is assessment. You are monitoring, observing, asking questions and gathering information for future instruction. You are also getting to know your students and how to personalize lesson plans, attend to their needs.

And you are teaching one-on-one in these moments (differentiating), but this is not the typical teaching that you might do by preparing a slide-show or writing a lesson plan. You must, in the moment, have a few tools you can draw upon. In these conferring moments, I draw from learning theory and psychology to help. As a former social worker, solution-focused conversations access schemas (prior knowledge and life experience) to stimulate ways of thinking that are self-reflective, productive, context-based, and autonomy-geared.

Coach Inferential Thinking: Nurture Complexity

Below are a few thought experiments to help engage your student-readers in more inferential thinking about their reading. Anchor these conversations in their reading. Ask for them to show you passages or sentences that support or stimulate their thinking.

Try "the miracle question." This is a goal-setting question when your student does not know how to imagine the future. Perhaps in your conference, a student wants to talk about a problem with a friend or family member. Now, you know that if it is serious that you should contact a school social worker, but this is stress about balancing school and work or this is about priorities or even self-doubt. Try this: *Suppose tonight, while you slept, a miracle occurred. When you awake tomorrow, you what would be some of the things you would notice that would tell you life had suddenly gotten better?* A follow-up question would be this: *How would that make a difference in your life?* The miracle question shifts the student from a problem-focused frame toward a visionary context. This questioning can also be used to focus on a character in the story if you would like to distance the conversation: *Tell me about a character in your book who is struggling. What would be their miracle, and how would that change things?*

The "empty chair." The empty chair was first popularized by Fritz Perls, a founder of gestalt therapy. This is an imaginative experience where the student imagines someone in a chair (a character, author, friend, historical figure) and begins a conversation. Then, the student imagines how the person would respond, taking up the chair from a different perspective. This engages the sometimes passivity of a student and encourages perspective-taking and problem-solving in context because the student-reader must draw on context from the text in order to engage in these conversations.

"**Voice Dialogue.**" If a student is reading a novel, there is a good chance that a character is feeling ambivalence or has doubt about things they've done or might do (think Prince Hamlet, Dally from *The Outsiders*). You might help the student-reader articulate that by saying something like: *It sounds like the main character is torn. On one hand, he wants....but on the other side, there is...How would you talk to the first side of this character? What would you say is driving this side? Now, let's move to the other side. What would you say to that side of the character?* This separates the selves of the character and encourages a closer examination of meaning but also a consciousness of the complexity of human decisions. What you are talking about is motive but also personality and relationships that pull at characters (and our students). This strategy can really help students (and teachers) understand choices and implications for characters.

"**Head-on Collision**" **conversation**: Another question you can pose during the reading conference is for those characters who are highly resistant or single-minded in seemingly self-defeating ways. This conversation begins with a summary: *Let's take a look at what's happening here. The characters says they want X, but every time they have a chance to move closer to that, they do something to mess it up.* Some questions you can pose include the following: How might the character be distancing themselves from people who want to be close? What decisions has the character made that have been destructive — what pain, loss, or suffering has the character experienced because of it? What trauma in the past is the character clinging to or making it difficult to trust? What does the character need to heal? What do you think the author will create in the plot to help this (or not)?

In each of these thought-experiments, the student is encouraged to infer and see how reading, at the secondary level especially, is about something more than identifying plot elements. Reading conferences at the high school level must match the development of the students who are now more capable of abstract reasoning (Piaget) and identity exploration (Erikson).

In some of these conversations, the student may share stories of their own life, connecting to or empathizing with the main character in the story. You will learn a lot about the student as a reader and human being, be sure to listen and remember the best follow-up statements: *tell me more* and *what makes you say so.*

Another note about reading conferences. Go to the readers. Whisper. Spend just a few minutes with each. Move on. You can probably talk to a few each day. Then, jot down some notes about what you talked about. I like to keep a notebook with one page for each student and just work my way through the pages each week, a technique suggested by Penny Kittle.

Next time your students are reading in class, use that time to do some personalized instruction in the form of conversation. This is formative assessment in its most beautiful and humane form.

The Answer to Vocabulary Instruction

Indeed, you read that article correctly. I wrote a "the" and not an "an." After fifteen years of teaching ELA in junior high and earning a doctorate in English focusing on literature, specifically genocide literature, I think I have found "the" answer. I practice this every day, but it only occurred to me to write about vocab after seeing a few posts in teacher discussion groups on social media. "How do you do vocab?"

Academic Vocabulary Instructions

There are many books on vocabulary instruction. I was first introduced to Marzano in 2004, my first year teaching and the early years of No Child Left Behind. Our school district purchased a copy of Building Background Knowledge for Academic Achievement for every teacher in our school district. The emphasis at the time in education was, well, "building background knowledge," which assumed to a degree that students did not have backgrounds. Still, the instructional approach being delivered to teachers and then to our students was "direct vocabulary instruction" as a way of " building academic background knowledge." The "academic" was the key here, and Marzano offered multiple appendices with terms for every subject.

Essentially, Marzano's theory of vocabulary instruction rests on teaching what he calls "singular" terms as opposed to "general" terms. To understand the relationship between vocabulary and background knowledge, he explains that "individuals naturally tend to think of specific referents even for general terms" (34) and students tend to process the meaning of a singular term from their personal memory unless the context directs us. If we read "disaster," what comes to mind stems from our personal memory (something we read, saw, or experienced) rather than a specific disaster (government shutdown, Hurricane Katrina, Chicago's Polar Vortex). Instruction shifts all learners to a common referent, the one within the context of the unit or the context the teacher determines should be common.

Any observer in our building would know our school used Marzano's work at the time because every classroom had a word wall, and many teachers were following Marzano's "six steps to effective vocabulary instruction": 1) teacher provides description, explanation, or example of the term; 20 students restate it in their own words; 3) students construct a picture/symbolic representation or act it out; 4) teacher extends and refines understanding with activities; 5) periodically discuss the terms; and 6) involve students in games to play and reinforce terms. If you look on Pinterest, you can see lots of graphics of this; almost one step for each day of the week. And you will see beautiful images representing referents drawn by students for their step 3.

Direct Vocab Instruction and Nuance

As a new teacher, I tried open and closed word sorts at the beginning of an instructional unit, pre-teaching all the words I thought they wouldn't know. We started vocabulary notebooks, that we neglected to update. I made quizzes and games and a lot of assumptions in selecting these terms. I did my best to control the imagery and understanding of these words; I watched students edit their drawings after seeing another student who had a more "right" referent. Still, students struggled to grasp abstract terms and concepts of literature and writing this way.

Literary concepts and writing ethos resist words and images in a vocabulary notebook; the key to understanding is nuance. I found relying on direct instruction undermined direct experiences of the art and humanity in the acts of reading and writing. Relying too much on lists and protocols as apart from the text means that indirect and nuanced "instruction" were pushed to the margin in our efforts to target a weakness in our state data and systematically respond with a research-based, measurable intervention. The six steps, word walls, lists, and quizzes of terms gave the district (and teachers) something tangible to do to improve test scores. Now with Quizlet and Google Forms that grade your multiple choice quizzes, digital tools may further remove the nuance and context of the art in our subject matter.

Theme and characterization don't make sense without characters, a story, and a reader. Syntax and diction resist comprehension without a writer and purpose. Sure, we can define the terms, but is that instruction? Meaning for the learner cannot happen until the reader experiences the story, interacts with the characters, crafts prose or verse. This is Rosenblatt's theory of reader response that is essential to comprehension; Rosenblatt values deeply the reader's schema or background knowledge. She does not view it as an empty vessel to be filled. Still, every teacher knows and understands when some part of our students schema conflicts or interferes with meaning. And here, the teacher or (better yet) peer-readers work through such nuance, interpretation, and significance in a discussion.

The Language-Conscious Classroom

Pre-teaching, pre-selecting vocabulary tends to minimize the background knowledge and life experiences within our students that could enrich their learning and the learning of their peers (and teachers) if we were to design our classrooms in such a way that we could regularly access their expertise and make visible the connections to content. Reading, talking and listening to others, exploratory writing and sharing — these are all ways we can nurture a language and experience-rich classroom.

During choice reading and writing, raising awareness about a word's connotation is one way you can intersect language and lives; every day, we do a quick-write, one of the options is to "write into a word" to uncover the story or meaning in the student's desired context. See my post "Almost 100 Quickwrites." Students are not required to write about the word, but we discuss it and then the students who do write about the word share it later in the week or month in our open-mic, so the word comes up again and triggers recognition.

When discussing literary terms such as characterization, it is helpful to consider words authors use to describe characters directly. In our weekly blog post, students identify passages to support their claims and then unpack the words in the quote, discussing connotation. This weekly practice brings readers closer to the word choice, author's craft, and, again, denotation and connotation. Image 1 shows a short but impactful assignment to study a word or phrase in the reading.

In a whole class reading experience such as poetry readings, *The Outsiders,* and *A Christmas Carol* (for our seventh grade classes), students encounter context-specific (time period) terms that may or may not trigger singular or general referents for readers. Students may rely on any memory they have close to that word. For misanthrope, they may see *ant.* For *pansy,* they may see pants. In many cases, a student can read past these words and get the gist or meaning of a passage, but these are places where an activity may be of use.

Quote: "But they were books. In this incredibly dark place, they were a reminder of less somber times, when words rang out more loudly than machine guns" (Iturbe, 26).

"Incredibly dark" shows that Auschwitz, for many people, is a symbol of death, doom, and darkness, giving the camp a negative connotation. The word "reminder" is showing that many people felt nostalgia and longed for the past, when there was peace, which is negative, but has a small ring of positivity in it. "Less somber times" also shows that the camp is dark and gloomy, also having a negative connotation. Finally, "words rang out more loudly than machine guns" shows the power of words, which shows the theme, where books penetrate the overall hardness and bleakness of the camp, which has a positive connotation.

Figure 1. Student interpretation of a quote from The Librarian of Auschwitz (Iturbe, 2012)

For *The Outsiders*, I asked students to make a sticky note for several context-specific words to note the connotation, identify if Ponyboy, the narrator, is uttering the word or if another character, and then lookup the words after concluding the chapter to reflect on how the denotation impacted their understanding. Of course, they do not do this in their daily choice reading (unless they wish), but this class practice for our shared reading is helpful in illuminating the simple fact that there are words that "are" the context. Any text in this anthology is great for a whole-class study of language use. See Image 2 for sticky notes.

To extend whole-class word study to independent reading, let's look at conferring during choice reading time. (See the section on conferring.) One student called me over for a conference to talk about a word: "adjutant."

We read the passage together. Noted that an officer was talking and that another was entering the room. One was a superior. I recognized the "adju" from my work as an adjunct instructor, but the student was stumped; we only knew for sure that it was used with a negative, almost insulting tone, and that was enough to go on. Still, the student wanted to know, and so after reading time, he looked it up: "a military officer who acts as an administrative assistant to a senior officer."

Will he ever see this word again? Perhaps. Will he use it in a story he writes someday? Likely. Should I have done a class mini-

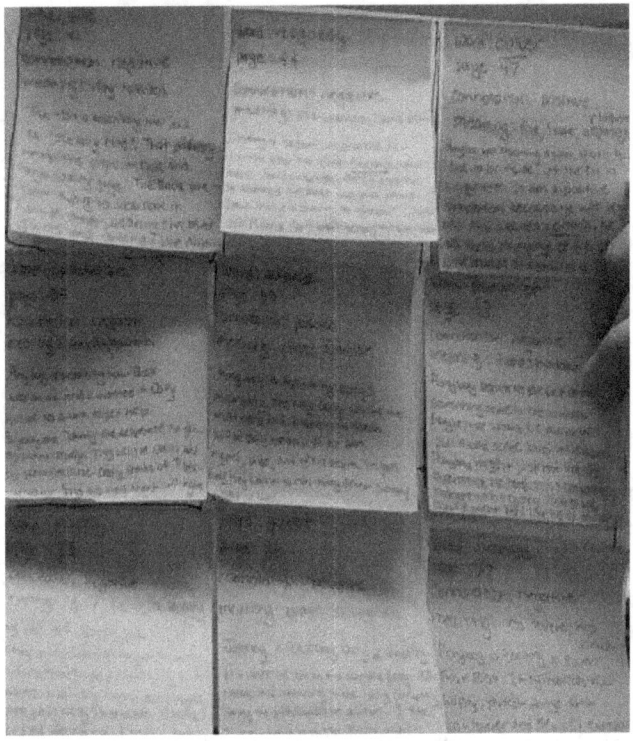

Figure 2 Sticky notes connotation study.

lesson on this word, made them draw a picture about it, add it to a class vocab list, test everyone on this one word? No. Do I now feel a bit worse about my title as an adjunct teacher? Yes.

As another example with poetry, let's look at our poetry Friday lesson. I recommend you set up a routine to read a poem, story, or essay from this anthology as a routine. In my classes, on Fridays, we did poetry readings.

One week, two students presented "Maestro" by Pat Mora and guided their peers through a close reading. This was before *Just YA* came to be. Students noted unfamiliar and important words in the poem. While the Spanish words were unfamiliar to some, context clues and cognates — "guitarra" and guitar, violin and violin— supported comprehension. And students knew that, in context, "voz" was musical. Still, a quick dictionary search confirmed what students inferred. No need to teach these words prior to reading the poem; the context, the deep reading, the synthesis among readers illuminates meaning (along with access to an online dictionary for some). See Image 3.

Both cast their music in the air
for him to snare his strings,
Songs of *lunas* and *amor*
Learned bit by bit
She'd nod, smile, as his bow slid
note to note, then trio
    voz, guitarra, violin
would blend again and again
to the last pure note
sweet on the tongue.

Lunas is Spanish for moon. It seems symbolic for the culture. It also means eternity and how family will always last forever.

Amor means love in Spanish. That shows the closeness between his family and the gratitude he has towards his parents.

	Claim/Answer	Evidence: quote from the poem (line 5)	Explanation of how the evidence proves the claim
:aker	The speaker is watching the	"Rows of hands clap	It shows specific observations

Figure 3. Student analyzing poetry on a Google doc.

In Closing

With 180 students reading a variety of books, poems, short stories, and essays, I cannot pre-teach vocabulary or create vocabulary lists that would meet the needs of all students. I cannot spend our 42 minutes of reading class going through the six steps of direct instruction. That is not "the" way.

So what is "the" way? Students. Let the context guide the process. Validate your students' lives as able to make sense. Teach that authors/poets help readers understand the meaning of a word not in the word itself but in its use, interaction with other words and the characters/humans using them. Dig deeper into a word as inspired to do so. Vocabulary instruction should not be a separate item on the lesson plan; no more "how do you do vocab?" Language is what we do; our singular and general; my referent and yours.

Four Quarters of Choice Reading: A Progression

For the past few years, choice reading has been the foundation of my reading pedagogy because choice values students as human beings with a range of interests, experiences, and tastes and because choice shares the responsibility of teaching with all the readers and books in the classroom. I rely on the authors to start conversations about the world with students in the pages of the books they carry.

It is, in fact, true that you (teachers) can teach all of the standards and all of the natural ways real readers read when your students are all reading different books. And it is true that book groups, whole class novels, essays, articles, poetry, and spoken word are also very important in a rich reading life — so, of course, there is more to reading instruction than choice reading. Still, each student will have a reading life to contribute to discussions, and he/she will be the expert on those books and those reading experiences. In other words, if the only texts students read in class are shared texts, then the conversations will be rather narrow and privilege the loudest voices.

All this said, when teachers have from 90 to 180 students reading different books, it can be difficult to track what everyone is reading and even more difficult to assess comprehension, emotional reactions, and the identification and interpretation of author's choices.

Documenting reading responses — written, verbal (in person/recorded) — is the best way I have found for me to assess students' reading and for students to self-assess and set goals for their personal reading lives.

I have found that when students notice trends in their reading choices that they will make slight adjustments and be more willing to try new books.

I have also noticed that regular feedback on what students are noticing when they are reading will 1) promote a deeper appreciation for author's craft and 2) improve meta-cognitive tendencies (or make them more aware or conscious of the many features of a rich reading life).

Reading response feel a lot like reading logs, but there is no parent signature or counting of minutes for a grade. The students must also own their progress. Too much monitoring creates a negative association with reading, so finding a balance of how and when to respond to reading takes constant revision.

I offer here four different ways I have conducted reading responses and supported students in tracking their reading choices. The *most* important component is the modeling and practice during class time. This is practice. I do not assess the practice. What I do not have here are the portfolios that we do every quarter, which I do assess because the portfolio shows the trends, evidence of comprehension and interpretation, and reading patterns. The portfolio is owned by the students and narrated by them — their voices talking through their reading lives. Only after gathering the data can they see trends and set new goals.

The focus of this section is just to show how I tried to understand each student as a unique reader while teaching and assessing the standards: 1) Cite several pieces of textual evidence to support analysis. 2) Determine a theme and analyze its development. 3) Analyze how particular elements of a story interact (setting shapes character or plot). 4) Determine meanings of words and phrases including figurative and connotative meanings. 5) Read and comprehend a RANGE — widely and deeply — from diverse cultures and different time periods with various text structures.

First quarter reading responses:

Model Noticing Author's Craft: Model how to create and use the Google Form to track their reading pace, choices in genre and text structure, and response (see video below). Show students how you think about the text and use reasoning and evidence to think through this.

Homework: Over the years, I assigned less and less homework, but we recognize that some schools do require this. Expect two or more additional responses at home for practice. Please avoid reading logs or parent signatures, which create a surveillance tone. Give feedback on one a week in class and adjust the modeling instructions to tweak the quality of reading responses. While students are reading, do NOT read, too. Instead, use this time to check in with students to praise their reading progress or offer suggestions/revisions. See the conferring section here.

Evidence Form (QR code): Each student should make his/her OWN Google form or survey form so that they are in control and have ownership of their reading life/record. Model how to set this up and use it yourself. Talk about what it is like to document your reading and what feels useful or intrusive. Have students share their form with you and insert a link to their form for you on a class hyperdoc roster. (See below for screenshots; click the link for an example.)

Image 1. Show the range of genre/form options.

Genre *

☐ mystery fiction (mysterious death or crime, suspects, detectives (professional or amateur)

☐ fantasy fiction (magic, supernatural, imaginary world with mage and magical beings, talking animals)

☐ science fiction (set in space, technology advanced, time travel, major social or world changes, dystopia, other plants)

☐ realistic fiction

☐ historical fiction (fiction, set in the past)

☐ graphic (comic, manga, informational, novel)

☐ verse novel or poetry book

☐ biography, autobiography, memoir (a person's life, nonfiction)

☐ drama (play form)

☐ picture book

☐ classics

☐ horror

☐ informational (snakes, rats, science, philosophy, cooking, an event)

Image 2. Students can write their response within the form and select from a range of topics.

Response with text citation (see response options) *

- The part where I was really **engaged** was ....because...
- **One subject** this book is explore is...and the character shows this by...
- **One word** that stood out to me was....and it means...in the context, which relates to the issue of ...in the book.

- **The thematic question** this book is explore is ....and one detail that supports this in what I read today is....
- In today's reading, ...**discovered**....because...
- **A wise quote or phrase** so and so said was .....because...

- **A powerful moment** or scene that got me thinking was...because...

- A character had to make a **decision** about ...because (what happened or who said something that provoked it).
- An **image or word** coming up again and again is....which means...
- Something cool or creative the author is doing in this part is....
- What is happening in the **plot** right now is...., which might be important because...

Image 3. A quick rating acknowledges not every reading experience is the same.

How would you rate your reading experience today? *

	1	2	3	4	5	
I struggled to focus and/or get into the book.	○	○	○	○	○	I found that I lost time. I was really into it; I found the flow today.

Responses practice: We recommend using class time to practice this response form. Model, practice, and assess how students do the following:

- Answer the question they've selected to ponder about their reading (see response stems below).
- Explain the answer (reasoning).
- Use *for example* or *because* to point to what prompted this thinking.
- Include a page number from the text (35) to show in-text citation.

Notice the response stems to help students with independent practice inspired by *Notice & Note* (Probst & Beers):

- What was something the character realized or hasn't realized yet? Why is that? How will this change things?
- What is something (an object, a word, a place, a conflict) that comes up again and again? What might this symbolize (love, hate, grief, the past, forgiveness, friendship)?
- What is a time when the character is remembering something in the past or the book flashes back? Why is this important to the character's personality, concerns, or the book's conflict?
- Think about a setting in your book. If you were in the setting, what are some things you might see?
- Describe an important event from your book and tell how it impacted different characters.
- Who is your favorite character in your book? Why is this character your favorite- personality, values, choices, interests?
- What do you think happened just before your story started? What about that created the opportunity for this story?
- If you could give the main character in your book some advice, what would you tell him or her?
- Is your book funnier or more serious? Why do you think so? What does the author do to make it so?
- What point of view is your book written in? How does it help you understand the thinking of characters?
- Do you like the main character of your book? Why or why not?
- Think of an important event in your book. How would the story have changed if this event had not happened?
- If you could ask the main character of this book three questions, what would you ask?
- Think about your book. Then finish this sentence: I wonder....
- Think of a new title for your book. Why do you think this is a good title?
- In what ways would this book be different if it were set 100 years in the past?
- What is the main conflict that the main character in your book must face?
- What are some important relationships in your book?
- Think about a supporting character in your book. How would the book be different if that character did not exist?

Over time, students will be able to see trends in their reading and then set goals to stretch their reading choices. Or maybe they decide they are ready for new authors or forms. See this snapshot of the form results after 15 entries.

Image 4. Google forms create charts for students to analyze reading patterns and set goals

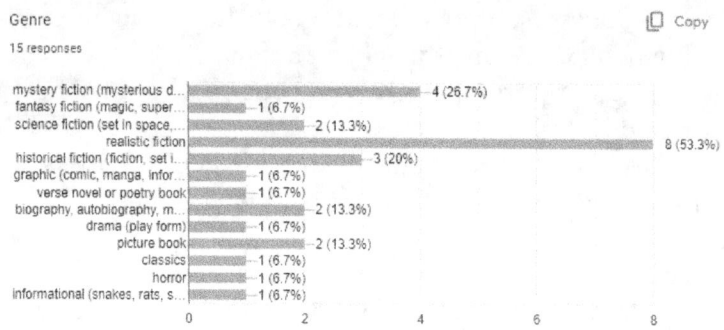

Second quarter reading responses:

The goal of this next quarter is to explore interpretation and meaning-making. However, you may find that second quarter may need another goal after looking at student forms.

Model making claims about texts: Using CER – claim, evidence, reasoning –model with your student another way of thinking about reading response. See Sarah's YouTube channel for a video on this.

Second quarter is not entirely different from quarter one, but it is a shift in thinking. Instead of talking about "what's going on in the book," readers are making claims about the implications of what is going on. This shift builds confidence in readers and opens up nuance as well. Practice CER with a common text — a short story or whole class novel. We read *The Outsiders*. (See chart below.)

Homework: Keep this the same as in the first quarter or adjust it as needed. I expected three (3) total responses a week on their evidence form, but we used class time for this rather than making it homework. I assessed just one entry. Give students feedback and then adjust your modeling to help students think deeply about the claims they are making. Emphasize that the reasoning should be the longest part of this response because you are more interested in hearing their thinking process. You can teach and model this during conferring time, too.

Evidence Form: Use the same Google form as the first quarter. You will really see a shift in the tone and insight in responses, but you may also see a decline in personal responses, so I added another column R – response to get students to think personally about the claim they made.

Response Format: CER(R) means claim, evidence, reasoning, and response. This is a scaffolded approach to literary analysis writing. The more students see this as a way of engaging with the text in lower stakes, daily reading and writing experiences, the less stressful longer literary analysis papers will be. Of course, this  structure supports book group conversations and whole-class Socratic seminar and fishbowl discussions, too. You can create a chart like this for students to paste into their reading notebooks or have a guide for during classroom discussions. We think *Just YA* is a great resource for teachers to model this process with any of the short texts and then welcome students to select texts to practice analytic writing or discussion. The QR is a video tutorial. Image 5 is an example of a CERR chart.

Image 5. CERR chart with examples from *The Outsiders*

Reading Response- CERR- Claim, Evidence Reasoning, Response by Sarah J. Donovan, PhD

Claim/Response: a debatable statement that can be supported with evidence (not a fact)	Evidence/Example Add a sentence that supports your claim.	Reasoning/Explanation Give your reasons for how the quote supports your claim and why this is important	Response
I noticed..., when... The effect of... on... is.. X believes.. The theme of this chapter is.. The setting change made the characters... The choice X made caused X to happen The way X reacted caused X to happen. The word X hints that X might happen. The most important word is X. When X happens, my heart/mind is moved. When X happens to X, I understand our world better When X happens to X, I understand my life better. X is a stereotype of... X defies stereotypes... Classism influences x Racism influences...	For example, the text states... Evidence from the text states... According to the text,...	If..., then... This proves... because. This supports my claim because	This book is teaching me ____because____ My favorite part so far is ____because____ I can connect to ___personally because ____ This book is making me feel ____because____ What I am learning about (life, society, humanity, [a topic] is ...
There is more to Dally than just causing trouble.	For example, Dally is really protective of Johnny. When Johnny confronts him at the drive-in, Dally wants to fight but doesn't. He says, "What did you say? What did you say to me? (16).	Therefore, Dally can regulate himself if he wants to. He just needs a good reason -- like the gang pet, Johnny	I am understanding how some friends can be more like siblings, especially when people don't feel loved at home.

Third quarter reading responses:

Model how to personalize the responses by giving students a range of methods for sharing their reading experiences. They are likely over the Google form responses, so here are a few ideas:

- Vlog (see the section in this book)
- Quotemaker (design quotes from the text followed by explanations)

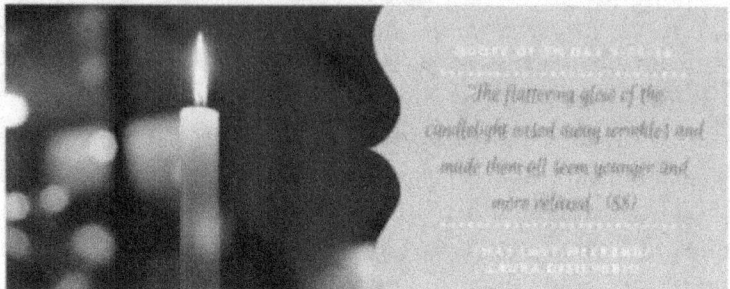

Today I read *That Last Weekend* from cover to cover. It was a mystery book and was actually pretty scary. It's mainly about these five college friends who spent one weekend together for a decade at a castle. And that's when something really bad happened. Ten years later, the main character, Laurel, goes back to the castle for the first time since the tragedy because she wants to find her four college friends which she hadn't seen since the tragedy. When Laurel is at the castle, a murderer attacks, and the five friends think that there is a murderer near them. This book really symbolizes friendship and how friends will do anything for each other. I chose this quote for today because it shows that, even in an unsafe, scary, murderous environment, if you're with your friends, you will feel safe. This quote summarizes the symbol of friendship with the candlelight. When I think of a candlelight, I think of peace, safeness, and togetherness. All of these bring the five friends together to solve the mystery of who the murderer is.

- Booksnaps (picture of the page of a book with a box around a quote and thought bubbles explaining it)

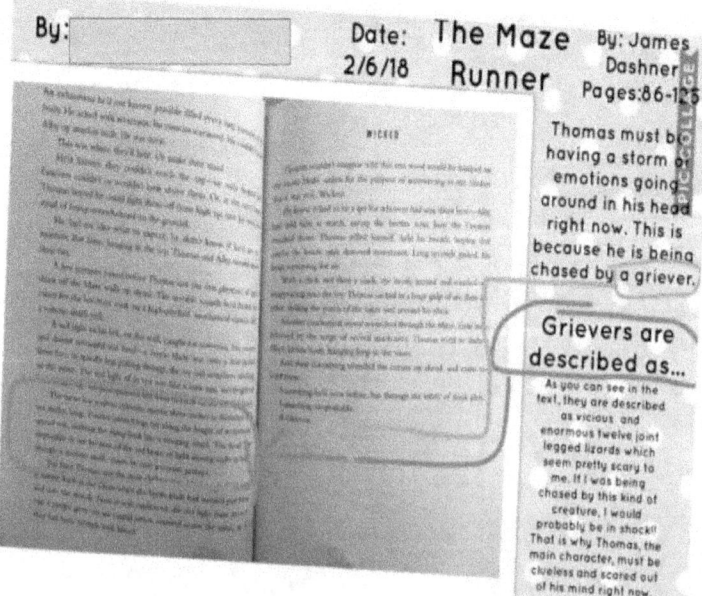

- Journal/Diary (doc, slides, or pictures of a notebook to discuss your reading)
- Blog (typed directly into the body of the blog)

Homework: Ask for one response during the week and one on the weekend. Again, you may abandon this altogether and use class time for the responses. Definitely, make time for the one during the week so that you can support and offer feedback. Assess the one they do independently and give feedback on that, too.

Evidence of learning: You will no longer use the Google form. Ask students to use the class roster hyperdoc to link to the site or place they will share their medium.

Response format: Students will do claim, evidence (quote) and reasoning, but with greater emphasis on the reasoning and response in their medium.

- Date of response
- Title of book
- Author's name
- Pages read since last response
- Claim: character, setting, conflict, author, symbolism, big issue, connections, great words, emotion
- Quote: text evidence with page (decide on APA or MLA)
- Explanation of what is going on in the book that helps us understand why this claim is important to think about as a person, a reader.
- Analysis of what key words mean in the quote denotation and connotation
- Analysis of how the words in the quote prove your claim.
- State your opinion, connection, emotional response, reaction

Fourth quarter reading responses:

For the final quarter, you may want to ease up on tracking reading, though students are likely keeping track and are amazed by their range of reading now that is visible in Google forms or a notebook list. Use this quarter to reflect on what they've read: authors, genres, forms, topics, and make some decisions to stretch or fill-in gaps. Use this time for students to make recommendations to one another. You should do the same.

Students will be very comfortable talking about the author's craft and genre and form. They will know all the literary elements and how various plots and structures impact their hearts and minds.

This quarter is a great time to review the reading life in the past year, so you can ask students to do a portfolio.

Students will create a comprehensive portfolio documenting their reading journey throughout the school year. This project will culminate in a presentation that reflects on their growth as readers, the impact of the stories they read, and their overall relationship with reading.

Components of the Portfolio:
1. **Reading Forms**:
    - Reading form or chart of all books, stories, genres, and poems read throughout the year.
    - Include the title, author, genre, and date completed.
    - Add a brief summary and personal reflection for each entry.
2. **Favorite Reads**:
    - Select a few favorite texts and create a slide or video segment for each, explaining why these were significant.
    - Discuss what they loved about these texts, any memorable quotes, and how these reads affected them personally.
3. **Stretch Texts**:
    - Highlight texts that challenged their reading habits or expanded their understanding of literature.
    - Reflect on how these texts stretched their thinking and reading skills.
4. **Learning and Exploration**:
    - Identify stories that taught them something new or prompted further learning.
    - Include any research or projects that stemmed from these readings.
5. **Poetry Exploration**:
    - Choose favorite poems and explore more works by the same poets.
    - Reflect on what drew them to these poems and any themes or styles that stood out.
6. **Recommendations**:

- ○ List books and stories they recommended to others and those recommended to them.
  - ○ Reflect on the impact of these recommendations and any discussions that ensued.
7. **Reading Reflection Essay**:
   - ○ Write a short essay about their relationship with reading.
   - ○ Discuss what it means to have a "just reading life," including access to stories, time to read, space to think about reading, and people to discuss reading with.
   - ○ Reflect on how these elements have shaped their reading journey over the year.
8. **Quotes and Reflections**:
   - ○ Collect favorite quotes from their readings.
   - ○ Write brief reflections on why these quotes stood out and how they relate to their reading experiences.
9. **Presentation**:
   - ○ Create a slide deck or video summarizing the key elements of their reading portfolio.
   - ○ Include visual and multimedia elements to enhance their presentation.
   - ○ Present to the class or a smaller group, sharing insights and highlights from their reading journey.

Final Compilation:
- Allocate time towards the end of the year for students to finalize their portfolios.
- Provide resources and support for creating the slide deck or video.

Presentation and Celebration:
- Organize a presentation day where students showcase their portfolios.
- Celebrate their reading achievements with a class discussion or a small event.

Evaluation Criteria:
- **Completeness**: Inclusion of all required components.

- **Depth of Reflection**: Thoughtfulness and depth in personal reflections and essays.
- **Creativity**: Creativity in the presentation format and visual elements.
- **Engagement**: Engagement with the reading materials and the portfolio project.
- **Presentation Skills**: Clarity and effectiveness in the final presentation.

This portfolio project aims to foster a love for reading, encourage critical thinking, and celebrate students' diverse reading experiences throughout the school year.

Vlogging as Embodied Reading Response

In an era where digital media is increasingly central to how we communicate and share ideas, vlogging has emerged as a powerful tool for self-expression and storytelling. Originating in the early 2000s, vlogging (a portmanteau of "video" and "blogging") quickly gained popularity as a platform for individuals to share personal experiences, insights, and creative content with a global audience. Today, platforms like YouTube, TikTok, and Instagram have transformed vlogging into a mainstream medium, accessible to anyone with a camera and an internet connection.

The Affordances and Benefits of Vlogging
Vlogging in the classroom offers a unique set of affordances that traditional writing assignments often lack. One of the most significant benefits is the opportunity for students to develop their verbal communication skills. Speaking directly to an audience, even through a camera, helps students articulate their thoughts clearly and confidently. Additionally, the multimedia nature of vlogging allows students to incorporate visual and auditory elements, enriching their narratives and enhancing engagement.

Moreover, vlogging can make literature and other academic content more relevant and exciting for students. By allowing them to create content that they can share with their peers or even a wider audience, vlogging fosters a sense of ownership and pride in their work. This public aspect of vlogging also encourages students to think more critically about their content, as they know it will be viewed by others.

Another key benefit is the development of digital literacy skills. In today's digital age, being able to navigate and utilize various technological tools is crucial. Vlogging requires students to learn and apply skills in video production, editing, and online publishing—competencies that are valuable in both academic and professional contexts.

Cautions and Considerations
While vlogging presents numerous advantages, it is important to approach this activity with certain cautions in mind. First and foremost is the issue of privacy and safety. Students should be taught about the importance of protecting their personal information and being cautious about what they share online.

Educators must ensure that students understand the potential risks of digital exposure and implement strict guidelines to safeguard their well-being.

Another consideration is the accessibility of technology. Not all students may have access to the necessary devices or reliable internet connections outside of school. To address this, educators should provide alternative ways for students to complete vlogging assignments, such as using school resources or allowing time during class.

It is essential to balance the creative freedom of vlogging with structured guidance. Without clear objectives and evaluation criteria, students may struggle to produce meaningful content. Providing detailed instructions, sample scripts, and evaluation rubrics will help students stay focused and ensure their vlogs are educationally valuable.

Incorporating vlogging into the classroom can transform the way students engage with literature and other subjects. By harnessing the power of digital media, educators can create dynamic, interactive learning experiences that develop students' communication skills, digital literacy, and critical thinking. However, it is crucial to navigate the potential pitfalls carefully, ensuring that students are safe, supported, and well-guided throughout the process. With thoughtful implementation, vlogging can become a vibrant and enriching component of modern education.

Vlogging as Embodied Reading Response
The integration of technology in the classroom has opened up new avenues for students to engage with literature in meaningful and dynamic ways. One such approach is through book vlogs, where students create video logs to discuss and analyze their readings. This method not only caters to diverse learning styles but also encourages students to articulate their thoughts, make connections, and deepen their comprehension. Here are the steps to successfully creating a book vlog, along with a sample script and evaluation criteria to guide your students.

Steps to Successfully Creating a Book Vlog (QR Code for handout)

1. *Read Widely*: Encourage students to read a variety of books, topics, and genres from their personal reading lists. This broadens their perspective and provides a richer base for their vlogs.

2. *Find a Quiet Space*: Advise students to find a quiet place in their house, neighborhood, or school where they can have uninterrupted time for about 10 minutes. If home Wi-Fi is inconsistent, they can sign up for library time at lunch or try a homework club. Note that class time may not always be available for this activity.

3. *Set Up the Recording Device*: Students should use their Chromebook or other devices, setting it up on camera mode with an app like Screencastify, Zoom, or another video app. They will also need their book and a few sticky notes.

4. *Choose a Claim*: Students should look over the provided claim options (see the list) and write one on a sticky note.

5. *Find Supporting Passages*: Have students mark one or two pages in the book that support their chosen claim with sticky notes.

6. *Start Recording*: Students should begin their Screencastify or Loom or phone recording, aiming for a video of no less than 8 minutes.

Sample Script

- Hello, my name is _____, and today is _____.
- Written by _____(author), the title of my _____ (genre) book is_____.
- (Hold up book)
- The pages I have read since last week are pages _____ to _____ (or say if you finished a book and started this one).

- What's going on in the book up to the plot point I want to focus on today is _____(who, where, when summary).
- Here is my claim _____ (see next page) that I want to discuss today.
- One passage that supports this claim is (read the passage).
- One key word in this passage is _____because _____(discuss the connotation, symbol, figurative meaning, tone).
- (Discuss character interaction, setting, class, culture, race, gender, etc dynamics that are happening to support your claim.)
- (If time...) Another passage that supports this is (read the passage); the key words in this passage are _____because _____
- The reason why these passages support my claim is because _____.
- As for my personal response to this section of the book, one joy I experienced was....because...., and another joy I experienced was... because...

QR Code for a sample video.

Support
To ensure students create thoughtful and comprehensive vlogs, provide them with the following evaluation criteria. Show them example videos by Alex, Nina, Grace, and Llyanna to illustrate the depth of reasoning and explicit and implicit analysis you expect.

Provide these sentence stems to support students in structuring their vlogs:

Claim/Thesis:
- I noticed... when...
- The effect of...on...is...
- X believes...
- The theme of this chapter is...
- The setting change made the characters...
- The choice X made caused X to happen.
- The way X reacted caused X to happen.

- The word X hints that X might happen.
- The most important word is X.
- When X happens, my heart/mind is moved.
- When X happens to X, I understand our world better.
- When X happens to X, I understand my life better.
- X is a stereotype of...
- X defies stereotypes...
- Classism influences...
- Racism influences...

Evidence:
- For example, the text states...
- Evidence from the text states...
- According to the text,...

Reasoning:
- The words in this quote like X shows...because...
- The quote relates back to something earlier when...which proves...
- These words caused X because...
- If X did not..., then... Therefore,...
- If X did not realize, then... Therefore,...
- This quote shows how ... caused/reacted/changed ... because...
- This quote made me think...because...so it relates to my claim because...

Response:
- Include your personal thinking, response, connections, opinion, concerns, and ideas about the world, humanity, and big concepts.
- Express what you are learning about the world or life through the characters and literature. Does the story sound familiar, or is it a life different from your own?
- Do you share any identity intersections with the characters? In what ways is the story a mirror for you, and in what ways is it a window (Bishop)?
- If the author is not an "insider" or you notice problematic scenes, might this be a "curtain book" (Reese) with distorted views?

By following these steps and utilizing the provided resources, students will be able to create insightful and engaging book vlogs that not only enhance their understanding of the texts but also develop their analytical and communication skills.

Vlog Evaluation Criteria

This single-point rubric, inspired by the *Cult of Pedagogy* website, is an asset-based assessment tool designed to support teachers in evaluating student work while promoting a readerly discourse.

By focusing on the quality and impact of various reading analysis moves, it facilitates meaningful conversations between teachers and students about literature. This rubric aligns with the *Just YA* anthology's goals, encouraging students to explore and discuss themes across its sections: being, love, land, world, futures.

Teachers can use this tool to enter grades and visibly demonstrate evaluation criteria, fostering a supportive and engaging learning environment.

Glow	Criteria	Grow
	TAG: Date, Title of book, Author's name & Genre, Pages read since last response or how far along in the book	
	Concise Summary: where, who, what, when (Somebody wanted...but...so...)	
	Claim Statement: literary element- character, setting, conflict, author's purpose, symbolism, social justice issue, connections to other texts, motif/language, emotional appeals	
	Passage(s): text evidence to support claim; read from the book TWO specific passages	
	Explanation of what is going on in the passage that supports the claims and "so what"-- why this matters within and beyond the text to readers	
	Critical Analysis: Get closer to zoom in on keywords for their denotation and connotation, implied meaning, connection to other text elements & the critical lens	
	Response: Share your opinion, connection, emotional response, a reaction related to mirrors/windows (Bishop) curtains/distortions (Reese), futures (Toliver), identity groups, humanity	

Concluding Thoughts

In closing, we hope this anthology not only brings joy and inspiration to your students but also becomes a cherished resource in your teaching toolkit.

By sharing these powerful stories, poems, and essays, you are introducing your students to the voices of our time and encouraging them to explore their own creativity.

We trust that this collection will ignite a lifelong passion for reading and writing, helping students see themselves reflected in the literature and empowering them to craft their own narratives that can shape the world around them.

Appendix

List by form.

Theme	Form	Title	Author
Just Being	Poem	A Place to Breathe	Christine Hartman Derr
Just Being	Poem	Bill-Bored	Glenda Funk
Just Being	Poem	Pitch Black	Stacey Joy
Just Being	Poem	Tracks	Karen J. Weyant
Just Being	Poem	High School	Joe Bisicchia
Just Being	Poem	North Dakota Snow Angels	Samuel Stinson
Just Being	Poem	Zit Ode	Stefani Boutelier
Just Being	Poem	How to Accept the Apology You Never Expected to Come	Hope Goodearl
Just Being	Poem	Wounded Healer	Darius Phelps
Just Being	Poem	My Voice	Melissa Heaton
Just Being	Poem	Cracking	Karen J. Weyant
Just Being	Poem	Bridge	Laura Shovan
Just Being	Poem	Step Father	Emanuel Xavier
Just Being	Poem	Hunger Is A Weapon	Federico Erebia
Just Being	Poem	Fragments	Laura Zucca-Scott
Just Being	Poem	Reality Bites	Rachel Toalson
Just Being	Poem	A Sweet-Smell Memory of School	Stacey Joy
Just Being	Poem	Psalms of My Broken Heart	Darius Phelps
Just Being	Poem	Let Me Tell You the Truth	Rachel Toalson
Just Being	Essay	On Being Armenian	Aida Zilelian
Just Being	Essay	Up Kahuna Road	Jonathon Medeiros

Just Being	Essay	Letter from Your New Psychiatrist	Dr. Sonia Patel
Just Being	Essay	Family Portrait in Scars	Kayla Whaley
Just Being	Essay	Slow Burn	Erin Murphy
Just Being	Essay	An Indian in Yoga Class: Finding Imbalance	Rajpreet Heir
Just Being	Essay	The Heroine	Rachel Toalson
Just Being	Essay	Crabby Hermits and Simone Biles: Using Satire and Experimental Forms	Carlos Greaves
Just Being	Essay	Zilelian from Zile	Aida Zilelian
Just Being	Fiction	Hot Lunch Petition	Aimee Parkison
Just Being	Fiction	The Blue Jay	Tamara Belko
Just Being	Fiction	The Reason	Val Howlett
Just Being	Fiction	This Story is Against Resilience, Supports Screaming As Needed	Jen Ferguson
Just Being	Fiction	Spontaneous Combustion	Kristin Bartey Lenz
Just Being	Fiction	Her Story	Padma Venkatraman
Just Being	Fiction	Get Ready With Me	Taylor Byas
Just Being	Fiction	Am I Okay?	Tamara Belko
Just Love	Poem	Daniel, My Brother	Federico Erebia
Just Love	Poem	Runaway	Emanuel Xavier
Just Love	Poem	landrover	Laura Kumicz
Just Love	Poem	Between Boys	Valerie Hunter
Just Love	Poem	Árbol	Emanuel Xavier
Just Love	Poem	Couples Skate	Karen J. Weyant
Just Love	Poem	Fill Me	Joe Bisicchia
Just Love	Poem	Graduation	Chris Crowe
Just Love	Poem	Haibun: My Girlfriend's House	Laura Shovan

Just Love	Poem	Alienated	Emanuel Xavier
Just Love	Essay	Remember	Jennifer Guyor Jowett
Just Love	Essay	Ready	Kate Sjostrom
Just Love	Essay	Twan't Much	Lee Martin
Just Love	Essay	Founding Haiku Festival	Regina Baiocchi
Just Love	Fiction	Bittersweet	Kennedy Essmiller
Just Love	Fiction	As Petals Fall on Asphalt Roads	Aimee Parkison
Just Love	Fiction	A Decent Human	Valerie Hunter
Just Love	Fiction	Natural Selection	S Maxfield
Just Love	Fiction	Promposal	Tamara Belko
Just Land	Poem	Thesaurus: Word Journeys	Jennifer Guyor Jowett
Just Land	Poem	Pebbles in My Palm	Jamie Jo Hoang
Just Land	Poem	Chase	Sandra Marchetti
Just Land	Poem	Herencia	Alicia Partnoy
Just Land	Poem	Inheritance	Alicia Partnoy
Just Land	Poem	The Queen of Bees	Kacie Day
Just Land	Poem	Witness	Sandra Marchetti
Just Land	Poem	Erased	Erin Murphy
Just Land	Poem	Jibaro Dreams	Emanuel Xavier
Just Land	Poem	(Mapping: A Key)	Jennifer Guyor Jowett
Just Land	Poem	La abuela y el mar	Alicia Partnoy
Just Land	Poem	The Grandmother and the Sea	Alicia Partnoy
Just Land	Essay	Living Near St. Catherine School	Jonathon Medeiros
Just Land	Essay	Stupid Girls	Jen Ferguson
Just Land	Essay	Swinging	Karen J. Weyant
Just Land	Fiction	Lights Out	Brittany Saulnier

Just Land	Fiction	The Stillness of Flight	David Schaafsma
Just Land	Fiction	The Listener	Aimee Parkison
Just World	Poem	Moonscape	Zetta Elliott
Just World	Poem	Juneteenth is Not Freedom	Stacey Joy
Just World	Poem	Girls' Playground, Harriet Island, St. Paul, MN (1905)	Jennifer Guyor Jowett
Just World	Poem	Belonging	Joe Bisicchia
Just World	Poem	We Gather Here Together	Rachel Toalson
Just World	Poem	Just Word(le)	Jennifer Guyor Jowett
Just World	Poem	Family Stories	Mary E. Cronin
Just World	Poem	There Must Be a Gate	Laura Shovan
Just World	Poem	I Refuse to Be Underestimated	Rachel Toalson
Just World	Poem	Unconstitutional	Stacey Joy
Just World	Poem	Peace Play	Linda Mitchell
Just World	Essay	Irish Whistle	Kate Sjostrom
Just World	Fiction	Feathers	Valerie Hunter
Just World	Fiction	Hunterlore	Dana Claire
Just World	Fiction	Drive-by (In Three Acts)	Jennifer Guyor Jowett
Just Futures	Poem	Chasing the American Dream	Laura Zucca-Scott
Just Futures	Poem	We Need Stories	Jennifer Guyor Jowett
Just Futures	Poem	Envision	Joe Bisicchia
Just Futures	Poem	A Remembrance	Rachel Toalson

Just Futures	Poem	Illuminated	Erin Murphy
Just Futures	Poem	Star Gatherers	Jennifer Guyor Jowett
Just Futures	Poem	Word of the day: Techwright	Stefani Boutelier
Just Futures	Poem	Don't Call Me A Robot	Laura Shovan
Just Futures	Poem	For Sale: M1k0 the Robot	Laura Shovan
Just Futures	Poem	MessageChatGPT	Linda Mitchell
Just Futures	Poem	Things Just Don't Work Like They Used To	Darius Phelps
Just Futures	Essay	A Vision for Inclusive Campuses: Balancing Comfort and Conflict Through Dialogue	Alana Mondschein
Just Futures	Essay	Compulsory Service	S.
Just Futures	Fiction	My Jam Jar Ghost	Shih-Li Kow

About the Editor

Sarah J. Donovan's professional interests include ethical, inclusive curriculum, methods, and assessment practices in secondary English classrooms. She is a former junior high English language arts teacher of fifteen years and an Associate Professor of Secondary English Education at Oklahoma State University. She wrote *Genocide Literature in Middle and Secondary Classrooms* and the young adult novel, *Alone Together*. Sarah edited *Rhyme & Rhythm: Poems for Student Athletes* and *Teacher-Poets Writing to Bridge the Distance* and co-authored *90 Ways of Community* and *Words That Mend*.

About the Authors

Kristin Bartley Lenz is a writer and social worker in metro Detroit. Her young adult novel, *The Art of Holding On and Letting Go*, was a Junior Library Guild Selection and a Great Lakes Great Books Award honor book. You can find more of her writing at www.kristinbartleylenz.com.

Tamara Belko is a reader, writer and teacher. As a middle school English teacher and Power of the Pen Creative writing coach, Tamara has spent her career sharing her passion for reading, writing and poetry with her students. Tamara is the author of young adult verse novel *Perchance to Dream*.

Joe Bisicchia has nearly four decades of experience in language arts, from journalism and broadcasting, to teaching, marketing, public affairs, and poetry. An Honorable Mention recipient for the Fernando Rielo XXXII World Prize for Mystical Poetry, he has written four published collections of poetry.

Stefani Boutelier, Ph.D., is an Associate Professor of Education at Aquinas College in Michigan. She teaches courses for pre-service and in-service teachers focused on instructional design, diverse literacy, technology integration, and research methods. Her K-12 teaching was in Southern California before moving into teacher preparation.

Taylor Byas, Ph.D. (she/her), is a Black Chicago native living in Cincinnati, Ohio. She has authored two chapbooks and her debut full-length *I Done Clicked My Heels Three Times*, which has won multiple awards. She is also a co-editor of *Poemhood: Our Black Revivial*, a YA poetry anthology.

Dana Claire is an award-winning author whose stories explore identity, fate, and destiny in the crossroads of romance and adventure. Her love of romantic tension, the supernatural and non-stop action has elicited positive feedback from many readers, as their online reviews reveal her flair for spine-tingling action and unforgettable characters.

Mary E. Cronin is a poet, author, and Literacy Coach who lives on Cape Cod in Massachusetts. Her picture book biography of PFLAG founder Jeanne Manford, *Like a Mother Bear*, is forthcoming from Simon & Schuster/Atheneum. Her poetry has been featured in *The New York Times, Radical Teacher, Rise Up Review,* and in *Rhyme and Rhythm: Poems for Student Athletes.* She is represented by Lori Steel of SteelWorks Literary. You can reach her at www.maryecronin.com.

Christopher Crowe is an American professor of English and English education at Brigham Young University specializing in young adult literature. In addition to his academic work, Crowe also writes books for the young-adult market, including *Mississippi Trial, 1955*.

Kacie Day is a rising poet and author whose work explores the beauty and challenges of the human experience. She resides in rural North Dakota with her husband and son, finding inspiration in nature and her close-knit community

Zetta Elliott's poetry has been published in numerous anthologies. Her first YA collection, *Say Her Name*, won the 2021 Lion and the Unicorn Award for Excellence in North American Poetry. *A Place Inside of Me: A Poem to Heal the Heart* was named a 2021 Notable Poetry Book by the NCTE.

Federico Erebia, a retired physician, woodworker, author, poet, and illustrator, is the recipient of the 2024 Lambda Literary Award for Exceptional New Writer. His debut novel, *Pedro & Daniel* (Levine Querido 2023), has received awards and other critical acclaim. He lives in Massachusetts with his husband. Visit https://FJEbooks.com for more details.

Kennedy Essmiller is a queer writer who earned her MFA in Creative Writing at Oklahoma State University. Her short story, "Mountains" won second place in the University of Western Alabama's 2017 Sucarnochee Review Fiction contest. Her work is published in *Frontier Mosaic* and *The Good Life Review*. You can follow her on Instagram at @kennedywogan.

Jen Ferguson is Métis with ancestral ties to the Red River and white, an activist, a feminist, an auntie, and an accomplice armed with a PhD. She is the award-winning (and award-losing!) author of *The Summer of Bitter and Sweet, Those Pink Mountain Nights* and *A Constellation of Minor Bears*.

Glenda Funk taught English and speech communication. She serves on NCTE's Children's Poetry Awards Committee. Her poetry is featured in *Teacher-Poets Writing to Bridge the Distance: An Oral History of COVID-19* in *Poems* and *Rhyme and Rhythm: Poems for Student Athletes*. Glenda has written for *California English* and blogs at Swirl & Swing: www.glendafunk.wordpress.com

Hope Goodearl is a high school English teacher with a love for creative writing of all aspects, even if she has a love-hate relationship with poetry. She has previously published 6 other poems to various journals and magazines with the hope of one day publishing a full-length novel.

Carlos Greaves is an Afro-Latino engineer, writer, and filmmaker. His writing can be found in *The New Yorker, NPR, McSweeney's,* and his Substack newsletter, *Shades of Greaves.* His debut book, *Spoilers: Essays That Might Ruin Your Favorite Hollywood Movies* is available wherever you get your books.

Jennifer Guyor Jowett teases stories and writers into being. She is the author of *Into the Shadows,* a middle grade historical fiction based on true-life events, the creator of the #dogearedbookaward, and a defender of fierce girls. Jennifer is a 7th/8th ELA teacher in the mitten state.

Regina Harris Baiocchi is a composer, author, and poet. Her music is recorded and performed by renowned orchestras and acclaimed artists. Her byline appears in *Modern Haiku, Obsidian, Fire This Time,* and elsewhere. She wrote urban haiku, blues haiku, and at the gate of the sun. Regina's fiction includes Indigo Sound, Finding Déjà, and Scuppernong.

Christine Hartman Derr is a citizen of the Cherokee Nation of Oklahoma. She holds a Master of Fine Arts in Writing for Children & Young Adults from the Vermont College of Fine Arts. She runs the website PawPrintsInTheSink.com and is a contributor to an upcoming YA anthology from Heartdrum.

Melissa Heaton has taught for 24 years and currently teaches 8th grade English at Mapleton Jr. High School in Nebo School District. She is an active fellow of the Central Utah Writing Project. When she is not teaching or writing, Melissa enjoys baking, reading, and traveling to national parks.

Rajpreet Heir received her B.A. in English Writing from DePauw University and her M.F.A. in Creative Nonfiction from George Mason University. An assistant professor of creative nonfiction at Ithaca College, she now lives in Ithaca, New York. Rajpreet has work in *The Atlantic, The Washington Post, The New York Times, Teen Vogue, Brevity, The Normal School,* and others.

Jamie Jo Hoang is the daughter of Vietnamese refugees. She grew up in Orange County, CA — not the rich part. She is the author of *My Father, the Panda Killer* and *Blue Sun, Yellow Sky.* Her work has also appeared in TIME, SALON and TinyBuddha.

Val Howlett is a folktale lover, curious researcher, and bookish florist. Their fiction has appeared in *Lunch Ticket, Hunger Mountain,* and two anthologies: *Ab(solutely) Normal: Short Stories That Smash Mental Health Stereotypes* and *We Mostly Come Out at Night: 15 Queer Tales of Monsters, Angels & Other Creatures.*

Valerie Hunter teaches high school English and has an MFA in writing for children and young adults from Vermont College of Fine Arts. Her stories and poems have appeared in magazines such as *Cricket, Cicada, and Paper Lanterns*, and anthologies including *I Sing: The Body and Brave New Girls*.

Stacey Joy is a National Board Certified Teacher who has taught for 38 years in Los Angeles. Stacey is a self-published poet and has poems published in various anthologies: *Out of Anonymity, Savant Poetry Anthologies, Teacher Poets Writing to Bridge the Distance*, and *Rhythm and Rhyme: Poems for Student Athletes*.

Shih-Li Kow is the author of *Ripples and Other Stories* and *Bone Weight and Other Stories*. The French edition (translated by Frederic Grellier) of her novel, *The Sum of Our Follies*, won the 2018 Prix du Premier Roman Etranger. She lives in Kuala Lumpur, Malaysia. www.shihlikow.com

Laura Kuzmicz is a young writer who has just graduated with a BA in English Writing and Journalism from Aquinas College in Grand Rapids Michigan, her hometown. In her spare time, she writes fiction and poetry, mainly focusing on grief, magical realism, and unique femininity. Laura is also an aspiring screenwriter.

Sandra Marchetti is the author of two full-length collections of poetry, *Aisle 228* from Stephen F. Austin State University Press (2023) and *Confluence* from Sundress Publications (2015). She is also the author of four chapbooks of poetry and lyric essays. Sandra's poetry and essays appear widely in *Blackbird, Ecotone, Southwest Review, Mid-American Review, Fansided* and elsewhere.

Lee Martin is the author of fifteen books, including the Pulitzer Prize Finalist novel, *The Bright Forever*. He teaches in the MFA in Creative Writing Program at The Ohio State University and the Naslund-Mann School of Writing at Spalding University.

S Maxfield is a genderqueer, bi+, and disabled writer. Their flash fiction has been published by *WinC Magazine* and *Voyage YA* by Uncharted, and s/he has a short story featured in the anthology *We Mostly Come Out at Night* (Running Press, 2024). linktr.ee/essmaxfield

Jonathon Medeiros, former director of the Kaua'i Teacher Fellowship, has been teaching and learning about Language Arts and rhetoric for nearly 20 years with students on Kaua'i and he frequently writes about education, equity, and the power of curiosity. He believes in teaching his students that if you change all of your mistakes and regrets, you'd erase yourself.

Linda Mitchell is a family girl, school librarian and creative person. She hangs out with her laptop, scissors, glue and paper from discarded books to make crafts with two mischievous young cats. Her favorite game is cribbage. She has published in several journals and weekly to her Poetry Friday blog, A Word Edgewise.

Alana Mondschein (she/her/hers) is a third year student at the George Washington University Elliott School of International Affairs studying Middle Eastern Studies. She was the 2023-2024 Jewish Student Association Co-President and Israel Policy Forum Atid Fellow. Alana delivered the above speech at the GW Summer Institute on Antisemitism.

Erin Murphy is the author or editor of more than a dozen books, most recently *Fluent in Blue* (Grayson Books). Her work has appeared in *The Best of Brevity, Ecotone, The Georgia Review, Rattle, Women's Studies Quarterly*, and elsewhere. She is professor of English at Penn State Altoona. www.erin-murphy.com

Aimee Parkison has published eight books and won FC2's Catherine Doctorow Innovative Fiction Prize and North American Review's Kurt Vonnegut Prize. She is Professor of Fiction Writing at OSU. Her work has appeared in *North American Review, Puerto Del Sol, Five Points,* and *Best Small Fictions*. www.aimeeparkison.com

Poet and human rights activist Alicia Partnoy is the author, translator or editor of twelve books and the chapbook *Ecos lógicos y otros poemares*. Her work is published in Spanish, English, Hebrew, Turkish, Bangla, and French. Partnoy is best known for *The Little School: Tales of Disappearance and Survival*, about her experience as a "disappeared" in Argentina in the 70's. Partnoy is Professor Emerita at Loyola Marymount University in Los Angeles.

Sonia Patel is a psychiatrist and author of the Morris Award finalist *Rani Patel in Full Effect* and In the Margins Book Award winners *Jaya and Rasa: A Love Story and Bloody Seoul*. Her fourth YA novel, *Gita Desai Is Not Here to Shut Up*, will be published September 2024.

Darius Phelps is a PhD candidate at Teachers College, Columbia University. An educator, poet, spoken word artist, and activist, Darius writes poems about grief, liberation, emancipation, and reflection through the lens of a teacher of color, as well as experiencing Black boy joy.

Brittany Saulnier is on a quest to inspire readers to find their own connection to nature. She is inspired by nature's secrecy and often blends environmental science with whimsy. Her short stories have been longlisted for anthologies and competitions. In addition to writing, Brittany co-created the Read to Write Kidlit Podcast.

David Schaafsma is a Professor of English at the University of Illinois at Chicago where he directs the Program in English Education. He teaches courses in English teaching methods, and literature. He's the author or co-editor of six books and is in the process of writing more.

Laura Shovan is a Pushcart Prize-nominated poet and a middle grade novelist. Among her award-winning children's books are *The Last Fifth Grade of Emerson Elementary, Takedown,* and *A Place at the Table,* written with Saadia Faruqi. Laura is a longtime poet-in-the-schools. She teaches at Vermont College of Fine Arts.

Kate Sjostrom is a writer and writing teacher educator based in Oak Park, IL. Her work has been published in *Rhyme & Rhythm: Poems for Student Athletes, RHINO, English Journal,* and elsewhere.

Samuel Stinson began developing an interest in writing after he began reading the novels of R.A. Salvatore in 1994. These days, Samuel teaches English and writes for a variety of publications. His most recent publication is *Embodied Environmental Risk in Technical Communication,* co-edited with Mary Le Rouge.

Rachel Toalson is the author of *The Colors of the Rain, The Woods, The First Magnificent Summer,* and *Something Maybe Magnific*ent (Simon & Schuster, 2024). Her poetry has been published in print magazines and literary journals around the world. She lives in San Antonio, Texas, with her husband and six sons.

Padma Venkatraman's novels *The Bridge Home, Born Behind Bars, A Time to Dance, Island's End* and *Climbing the Stairs,* have secured over 20 starred reviews, won multiple awards and sold > 250,000 copies. Visit www.padmavenkatraman.com to read more about oceanographer-turned-author Dr. Venkatraman; contact The Author Village to arrange a visit.

Karen J. Weyant's first full-length collection, *Avoiding the Rapture* was published last fall by Riot in Your Throat press. Her poems have appeared in *Crab Orchard Review, Copper Nickel, Harpur Palate, Fourth River, Lake Effect, Rattle, River Styx* and *Slipstream*. She lives, reads and writes in Northern Pennsylvania but is an Associate Professor of English at Jamestown Community College in Jamestown, New York.

Kayla Whaley holds an MFA from the University of Tampa and is former senior editor of Disability in Kidlit. Her work has appeared in anthologies including *Unbroken, Vampires Never Get Old, Game On,* and *Allies.* She is also the author of chapter book series A to Z Animal Mysteries.

Emanuel Xavier is author of several poetry books including *Selected Poems of Emanuel Xavier* and *Love(ly) Child*. His books have been finalists for International Latino Book Awards and Lambda Literary Awards and his work has appeared in *Poetry, A Gathering of the Tribes, Best American Poetry,* and elsewhere.

Aida Zilelian is a first generation American-Armenian writer, educator and storyteller from Queens, NY. She is the author of *The Legacy of Lost Things* (2015, Bleeding Heart Publications) which was the recipient of the 2014 Tololyan Literary Award. Aida's most recent novel, *All the Ways We Lied*, released in January 2024 (Keylight Books/Turner Bookstore).

Laura Zucca-Scott, Ph.D., is a bilingual writer and educator. Her works have been published in English and Italian. Recently, her work was featured in the North Dakota Quarterly. In December 2023, she was the recipient of the Third Prize of the International Literary Prize, "Florence, Capital of Europe," Italy.

S. is a college student and English teacher in Armenia.

About the Advisory Board

Diana M Bayona (she/her) is a Colombian native who lives in Tulsa. She climbed the education ladder by entering the education field as an EL aide, moving into the classroom to teach first, second and Kindergarten, to be an EL Instructional Coach for elementary schools the last 6 years and this year moving her coaching skills to High School. She is an LLCE PhD candidate at OSU.

Henry "Cody" Miller is an associate professor of English education at SUNY Brockport. Prior to that role, he taught high school English in Florida for seven years.

Akira Park (she/her/siya) is an English Secondary Education major and a McNair Scholar at Washington State University. Her research interests include culturally sustaining pedagogy and BIPOC representation in young adult literature with a focus on Asian American narratives.

Sidra Zaheer is a second-year PhD student in Language, Literacy, and Culture at Oklahoma State University. As a Graduate Teaching Assistant, she teaches the undergraduate course "American Stories: Diverse Peoples in YA Literature." Sidra's background includes experience as an ESL and IELTS instructor, as well as teaching secondary students. Her research interests focus on innovative English language instruction, technology integration, and diversity in young adult literature. Sidra has presented at conferences on topics such as digital storytelling and gender representation in YA literature.

Lauren Vandever has been teaching middle school Reading and English for over 10 years. She has a Master's degree in Reading and Literacy instruction and is currently serving as an instructional coach in her district while pursuing a doctorate.

Laura Swigart (she/her) is a secondary educator in Oklahoma City, OK, and a Master's student at Oklahoma State University. She has taught for 8 years, and has served as an Instructional Coach and Professional Development leader, focusing on literacy strategies in content classrooms, and culturally sustaining pedagogy.

Robin Pelletier is a secondary educator in Las Vegas, Nevada where she's taught ELA for 9 years. Since 2019, she has been a professional reader for NetGalley. She has worked for Barnes and Noble for the past 3 years. She participates in many book studies, professional development trainings, and conferences, presenting annually at the Summit for the Research and Teaching of Young Adult literature with her students.

www.ingramcontent.com/pod-product-compliance
Lightning Source LLC
Chambersburg PA
CBHW060630260626
47161CB00008B/2854